sweetwater's
SIMPLE HOME

SEW SOMETHING HANDMADE FOR EVERY ROOM • 35 PROJECTS

Lisa Burnett,

Karla Eisenach &

Susan Kendrick

stashBOOKS.

an imprint of C&T Publishing

Publisher: Amy Marson

Creative Director: Gailen Runge

Acquisitions Editor: Susanne Woods

Editor: Cynthia Bix

Technical Editors: Janice Wray and Sandy Peterson

Cover/Book Designer: Kristy Zacharias

Production Coordinator: Jessica Jenkins

Production Editor: Alice Mace Nakanishi

Illustrator: Janice Wray

Flat Quilt Photography by Christina Carty-Francis and Diane Pedersen of C&T Publishing, Inc., unless otherwise noted; Style Photography by Farmhouse Creations, Inc., unless otherwise noted

Published by Stash Books, an imprint of C&T Publishing, Inc., P.O. Box 1456, Lafayette, CA 94549

Library of Congress Cataloging-in-Publication Data

Eisenach, Karla (Karla Gordon)

Sweetwater's simple home : sew something handmade for every room : 35 projects / Karla Eisenach, Lisa Burnett, and Susan Kendrick.

p. cm.

ISBN 978-1-60705-213-5 (soft cover)

1. House furnishings. 2. Machine sewing. I. Burnett, Lisa (Lisa Eisenach) II. Kendrick, Susan (Susan Eisenach) III. Title. IV. Title: Sew something handmade for every room : 35 projects.

TT387.E35 2011

646.2'1--dc22

2010051956

Printed in China

10 9 8 7 6 5 4 3 2

ACKNOWLEDGMENTS

A special thank-you goes out to everyone who helped make this book a reality. To C&T Publishing for letting us come up with an idea and run with it. To our fabric company, Moda, for allowing us to design fabric that stays true to our style. To Michelle Odle and Brian Clements for dropping everything to quilt a project that was due yesterday. To our families for putting up with and supporting every idea we dream up (and there are a lot of ideas). To our many loyal customers who followed us from quilting to scrapbooking and back again. Finally, to the kids of Sweetwater, Jordan, Bryce, and Cash. You are our inspiration.

DEDICATION

This book is dedicated to
everyone who has supported
us for so many years. . . .

To the shop owner who orders
our patterns,

To the mom who uses a Sweetwater
piece of patterned paper
in her scrapbook,

To the seamstress who chooses
our fabric for her next quilt,

To our blog readers who regularly
check to see what we are up to,

Thank you.

CONTENTS

Simple

adj.   clear, understandable; easy.

INTRODUCTION

The concept of the simple home is the exact opposite of the way we live our lives. There is little that is simple in the twenty-first century—that's why we seek out the uncomplicated, the clean, the simple.

Our homes can provide us with that simplicity. Surround yourself with things you absolutely love, that give you a sense of serenity. Personal, handmade items can give you that feeling of calmness as well as a sense of pride and accomplishment. Many people shy away from such endeavors, fearing the process will be difficult or complicated—anything but simple. This book is intended to show you that beautiful, handmade items can be easy to make. You can finish a project in an afternoon or a weekend. While we love intricate king-sized handmade quilts, we also love the instant gratification of completing a table runner on a relaxing Sunday afternoon.

Although too many things can clutter your home as well as your mind, we encourage you to have at least one handmade item in each room of your house. It can be as simple as your child's latest painting hung on the refrigerator door or handmade placemats set at your dining room table. Your style and personality will come through, and those simple things will make it *your* home.

They may not acknowledge it, but your family members will appreciate having things you actually made present in their lives. These handmade things will provide memories and a sense of history. No one will be fighting over a randomly purchased set of sheets, but the handmade pillow that lies on your bed will be cherished forever.

We hope this book inspires you to show off your personality and style in your home. Most of the projects were created with fabrics we designed ourselves, which, of course, is our style. Don't be scared to change fabrics and colors to fit your personality. Just keep it simple.

the ENTRYWAY

First impressions are everything. Not only does your entryway welcome guests, but it also welcomes *you* home. Make this space cozy and inviting. Lay a quilt over a vintage bench or chair, spruce up buckets with fresh flowers, and hang framed artwork or photos on the wall.

CIRCLE QUILT

| FINISHED QUILT: 51" × 51" |
| FINISHED BLOCK: 5½" × 5½" |

Designed and made by Sweetwater
and machine quilted by Brian Clements

The blue and brown color palette of this quilt is so calming, especially on a crisp fall day. For a different variation, try a summer version using brighter fabrics. Make the circles pop even more by using a light-colored neutral background behind colorful circles. Think citrus shades—orange, lime green, and pink.

INSTRUCTIONS

The pattern is on page 16; a ¼" seam allowance is included when constructing blocks and borders.

Blocks

This quilt has 25 circle appliquéd blocks and 24 plain blocks.

1. Cut 25 squares 6" × 6" from the circle block fabric.

2. Cut 24 squares 6" × 6" from the plain block fabric.

3. To make the appliqués, make a circle template from the pattern and trace around it 25 times on the paper side of the fusible web.

4. Iron the fusible web to the wrong side of the dot fabric, following the manufacturer's instructions.

5. Cut out the circles on the traced lines.

6. Peel off the paper backing and iron a circle to the center of each of the 25 circle block squares.

7. Machine stitch close to the edge of each circle using a straight stitch.

what you
need

FABRIC FOR CIRCLE AND PLAIN BLOCKS: 2 different prints, 1 yard each

FABRIC FOR CIRCLE BLOCK DOTS: ¼ yard

PAPER-BACKED FUSIBLE WEB: ½ yard

FABRIC FOR INNER BORDER: ¼ yard

FABRIC FOR OUTER BORDER AND BINDING: 1⅜ yards

BACKING FABRIC: 59" × 59"

BATTING: 59" × 59"

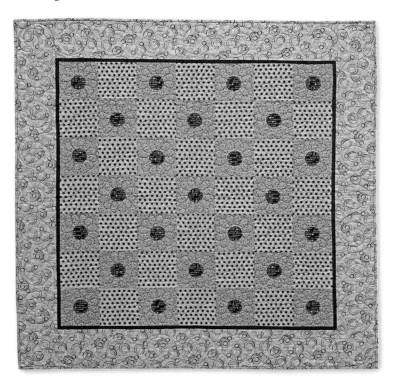

Quilt Top

There are 7 rows of 7 blocks each. Refer to the quilt assembly diagram (page 15).

1. Begin the first row with a circle appliqué block. With right sides together, sew 7 squares together, alternating appliqué and plain blocks, to make 1 row. Press all the seams toward the circle appliquéd blocks. Repeat 3 times.

2. Sew another row of 7 squares, starting this time with a plain block, alternating plain and appliqué blocks. Press. Repeat 2 times.

3. Sew the 7 rows together and press.

Borders

This quilt has an inner border and an outer border. Refer to Borders (page 136) to sew the strips to the sides, top, and bottom of the quilt.

1. Cut 4 strips 1″ × the width of the fabric for the inner border.

2. Cut 5 strips 6″ × the width of the fabric for the outer border.

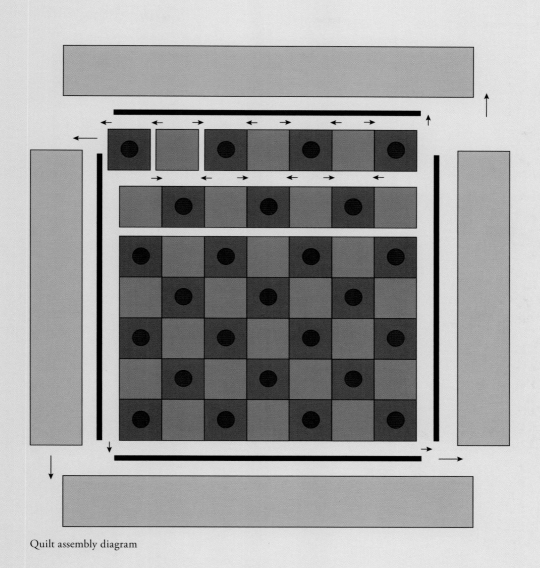

Quilt assembly diagram

Finishing

For the binding, cut 6 strips 2¼″ × the width of the fabric; sew them together using diagonal seams to make 1 long strip.

Refer to Basic Techniques (page 135) to layer, quilt, and bind the quilt.

Quilt your quilt top as desired. Our quilt features a flower pattern around each appliquéd circle and free-flowing swirls on the border and in the plain blocks.

Circle Quilt
Circle Pattern
Cut 25.

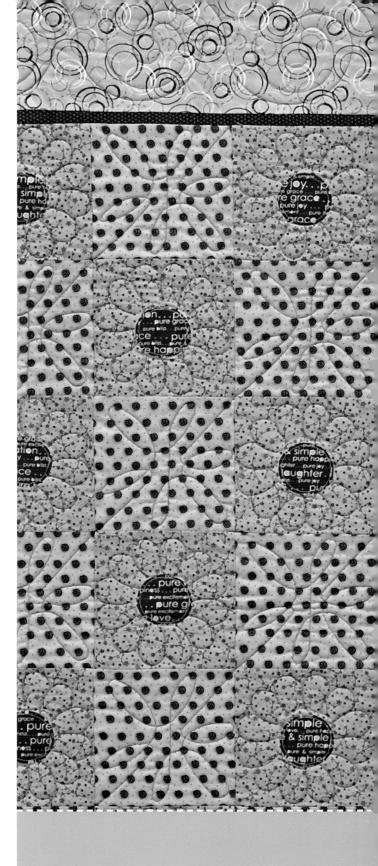

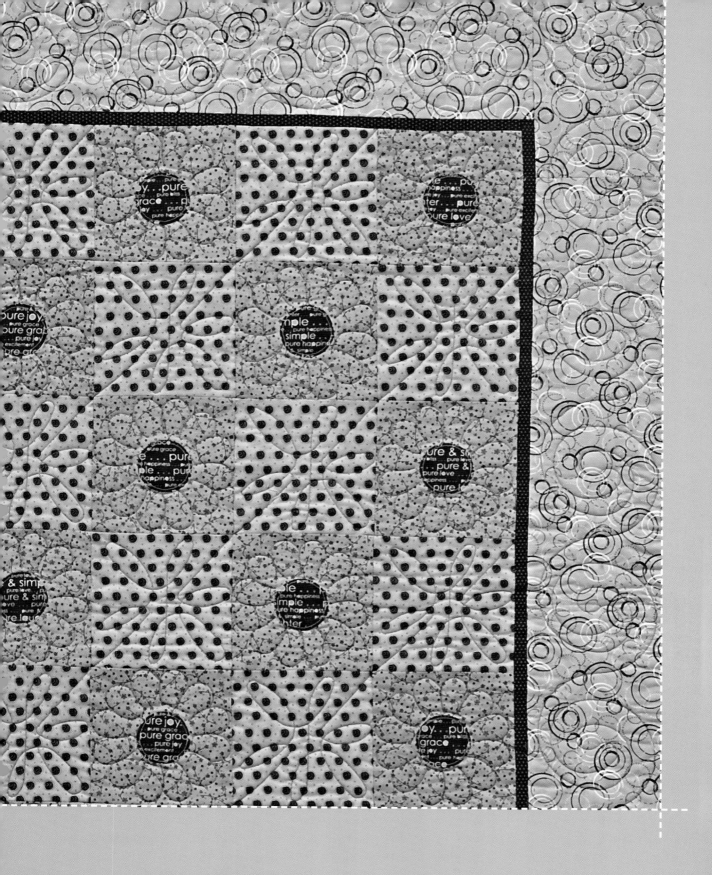

PURE PILLOW

Designed and made by Sweetwater

Sometimes the simplest things create the biggest impact. Choose a word that reflects the kind of atmosphere you want to create, and stencil it onto the pillow front. The simplicity of the pillow allows the word to be the focus.

INSTRUCTIONS

A ¼" seam allowance is included.

Stenciled Pillow Front

1. Cut 1 piece of fabric 16½" × 16½" for the pillow front.

2. To make a stencil from freezer paper, use your computer to print a word in the font of your choice, approximately 2" tall. For best results and ease of cutting, choose a bold sans serif font such as Arial Black.

3. Trace the word onto the nonshiny side of the freezer paper and carefully cut out the letters with scissors. Discard the letters.

4. Iron the shiny side of the freezer paper to the front of the pillow.

5. With a foam brush, use a dabbing action to paint over the stencil using acrylic paint.

6. Allow the paint to dry thoroughly (see the manufacturer's directions) and then pull off the freezer paper.

Pillow Assembly

1. Cut 2 pieces of fabric 12" × 16½" for the back of the pillow.

2. Turn the fabric under ¼" on a 16½" side of each piece. Press.

3. Turn the fabric under ¼" again. Press and topstitch in place.

4. With the right sides together, pin the front to the back pieces, overlapping the hemmed back pieces. Stitch a continuous seam all around, ¼" in from the edges.

5. Trim the corners.

6. Turn the pillow cover right side out, press, and insert the pillow form into the back opening.

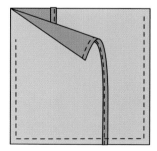

Overlap back pieces.

what you
need

FABRIC FOR FRONT AND BACK: ½ yard solid-color fabric

FREEZER PAPER, such as Quilter's Freezer Paper Sheets (by C&T Publishing), or alphabet stencils (available at craft supply stores)

ACRYLIC PAINT, such as Liquitex (by C&T Publishing)

SMALL FOAM BRUSH

16" × 16" PILLOW FORM

FINISHED BAG:
14″ wide × 11″ high × 3½″ deep

MARKET TOTE BAG

Designed and made by Sweetwater

Everyone knows that plastic bags should become a thing of the past. Help the environment by making this super-easy bag. Make sure to keep it close to the front door so you can grab it and go when heading to the market.

INSTRUCTIONS

A ½″ seam allowance is included.

Bag Body

1. Cut 2 pieces 15″ × 12″ from the bag body fabric for the front and back.

2. Cut 2 pieces 12″ × 4½″ from the bag body fabric for the sides.

3. Cut 1 piece 15″ × 4½″ from the bag body fabric for the bottom.

4. With the right sides together, sew the 2 side pieces to the bottom piece along the 4½″ sides to make 1 long strip as shown.

Side	Bottom	Side

Side/bottom strip

5. With the right sides together and matching the seams with the corners, sew the long side/bottom strip to the bottom and side edges of the front piece. Pivot at the corners, clipping the side/bottom strip as necessary.

6. Sew the side/bottom strip to the back piece in the same manner.

7. If needed, zigzag the seams to keep the edges from raveling. Turn the bag body right side out.

Lining

1. Cut the front, back, sides, and bottom pieces from the lining fabric, using the same dimensions as for the bag body pieces in Bag Body, Steps 1–3 (above).

2. To construct the lining, repeat the sewing instructions for the bag body, but do not turn the lining right side out.

3. Insert the lining into the bag body.

4. Baste the top raw edges together.

what you
need

BURLAP OR CANVAS FABRIC FOR BAG BODY: ⅔ yard

FABRIC FOR LINING: ⅔ yard

FABRIC FOR HANDLES AND FACING: ½ yard

1½″ ALPHABET RUBBER STAMPS (available at craft or scrapbooking stores)

ACRYLIC PAINT, such as Liquitex (by C&T Publishing)

Handles

1. Cut 2 strips 23″ × 4″ from the handles and facing fabric.

2. With the *wrong* sides together, fold the long edges of each strip to the center and press.

3. Fold the strips lengthwise again, matching the folded edges.

4. Topstitch close to both edges of each strip.

5. Pin the raw ends of each handle to the front and back top opening edges on the outside of the bag, positioned 3″ from each side seam.

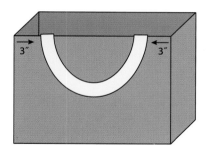

Handles are attached to both front and back of bag.

Facing

1. Cut 1 strip 2¼″ × 36″ from the handles and facing fabric.

2. With the right sides together, sew the 2¼″ ends together.

3. Turn one edge of the facing ¼″ to the wrong side. Topstitch close to the edge.

4. With the right sides together, sew the facing to the top opening of the bag, with the handles sandwiched in between and the raw edges even.

5. Turn the facing to the inside of the bag and press.

6. Topstitch close to the top edge through all the layers.

Stamped Words

1. Choose any word to stamp on the front of the bag.

2. Brush black acrylic paint on the rubber stamp and press firmly. Allow the paint to dry.

Helpful Hint

To center the word, count the number of letters in the word. Start with the middle letter and center and stamp it on the bag. Then add the remaining letters on each side of the middle letter.

ENTRYWAY ACCESSORIES

Dress up your entryway with very simple touches that start with purchased items.

These are old sap buckets that we bought at a garage sale, but you could use any kind of bucket or other container you like. We spray painted ours with chalkboard paint. Use chalk to write different words on them, depending on the season or your mood.

The frame pictured was purchased with the words already on it (see Resources, page 140). But you could replicate it by using rubber stamps and black ink on a plain white frame. To finish the project, sew buttons in a circular pattern on a favorite piece of fabric. Simply mount the fabric on cardboard and place it in the frame.

the KITCHEN

There's no place like the kitchen. It is truly the heart of the home. Whether you are flipping pancakes in the morning or your kids are raiding the refrigerator after school, the kitchen is always one of the busiest rooms of the house. Make yours special with handmade items that serve a purpose. The projects in this chapter are pretty to look at and useful at the same time.

NEWSPRINT
APRON   *Designed and made by Sweetwater*

This apron is so cute that you may want to hang it up and admire it instead of using it. Then again, wearing it could make any kitchen chore more fun.

INSTRUCTIONS

The pattern is on page 31; a ¼" seam allowance is included.

Neck Ties

1. Cut 2 strips 2" × 22" from the waistband and ties fabric for the neck ties.

2. Fold 1 short edge on each strip ¼" to the wrong side and press. With the *wrong* sides together, fold the long edges to the center and press.

3. Fold the strips lengthwise again, matching the folded edges.

4. Topstitch close to the folded edges around each strip.

Apron Top

1. Cut 2 pieces 12" × 10" of the main fabric for the apron top front and back.

2. Use the pattern to trace, enlarge, and cut 2 pieces of the scallop trim fabric.

3. With the right sides together, sew a scallop trim piece to each of the apron top front and back pieces along a 12" side.

4. Press the seams to one side.

5. With the right sides together, pin the short raw ends of the neck ties between the apron top front and back, positioned 1½" from the sides, with the neck tie and scallop raw edges even.

6. Sew the apron top front to the back along the sides and across the scallop, leaving the bottom edge open.

7. Clip the curves and trim the corners.

8. Turn the apron top right side out and press.

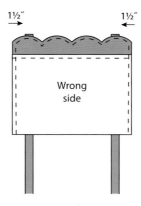

Sew apron top front to back.

what you **need**

MAIN FABRIC: 1 yard

FABRIC FOR WAISTBAND AND TIES: ½ yard

FABRIC FOR SCALLOP TRIM: 3" × width of fabric

FABRIC FOR RUFFLES: 3 different prints, ¼ yard each (minimum 42" wide)

Apron Skirt

1. From the main fabric, cut 1 piece 22″ × 22″.

2. Turn the edges of the fabric under ¼″ on the sides and bottom and press.

3. Turn the edges under another ¼″ and press.

4. Topstitch all 3 edges.

5. Sew a gathering stitch along the top raw edge of the skirt, and gather to measure 16″.

6. With the *wrong* sides together, pin the apron top to the apron skirt, matching the raw edges. Baste. The skirt will extend 2″ beyond each side of the top; the extra fabric will be sewn to the waistband.

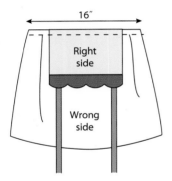

Baste gathered skirt to apron top.

Waistband and Ties

1. From the waistband and ties fabric, cut 3 pieces 3″ × 22″. With the right sides together, sew the 3 pieces together along the 3″ ends to make 1 long strip.

2. Turn the fabric edges under ¼″ and press.

3. With the wrong sides together, fold the band in half lengthwise, matching the turned-under edges.

4. Center and sandwich the seam allowance of the apron top and skirt between the 2 sides of the band with the long turned-under edges of the band aligned. Sew together, stitching close to the turned-under edges.

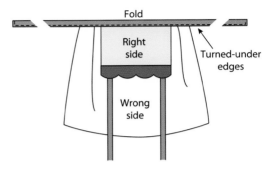

Stitch waistband and ties to apron top and skirt.

5. Turn the apron top up and baste the band to it. Topstitch along the folded edge of the band through all the layers.

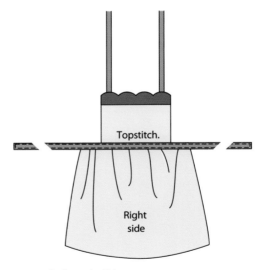

Topstitch through all layers.

Ruffles

1. Cut a strip 6″ × 42″ from each of the 3 ruffle fabric prints.

2. Hem 2 short edges and 1 long edge of each ruffle by turning the edges under ¼″ twice and topstitching.

3. Turn the fabric under ½″ along the remaining long raw edge of each ruffle and press.

4. Sew a gathering stitch ¼″ from the folded edge of each ruffle.

5. Gather the ruffles to fit the width of the apron skirt.

6. Sew the bottom ruffle to the skirt first. Place the top of the ruffle 4″ from the bottom edge of the skirt, and stitch over the gathering stitch.

7. Repeat Step 6 for the remaining 2 ruffles, except place the second ruffle 6″ from the bottom edge of the skirt and the third ruffle 8″ from the bottom of the skirt.

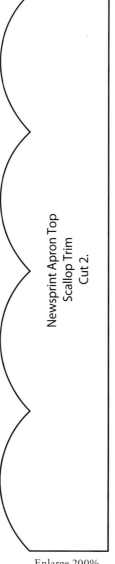

Newsprint Apron Top
Scallop Trim
Cut 2.

Enlarge 200%.

CIRCLE POT HOLDERS

Designed and made by Sweetwater

We love how the colorful binding of these pot holders really "pops" next to the black and cream fabric. They make great gifts—think teachers, grandmothers, and even your mail carrier. Who couldn't use a new set of pot holders?

INSTRUCTIONS

The pattern is below; a ¼" seam allowance is included.

1. Use the pattern to cut 4 quarter-circle pieces from the 4 prints.

2. With the right sides together, sew together 2 of the quarter-circles along a straight edge. Press. Repeat with the remaining 2 quarter-circles and press.

3. Sew together the 2 pieced half-circles to make the front. Press.

4. Layer the back, batting, Insul-Fleece, and front together.

5. Stitch close to the edge of the front through all the layers and trim away the excess back and batting.

6. Quilt the pot holder as desired. We used a flower design.

7. Refer to Continuous Bias Binding (page 138) to make and apply the bias binding. Cut bias strips 2¼" wide and measuring 30" long.

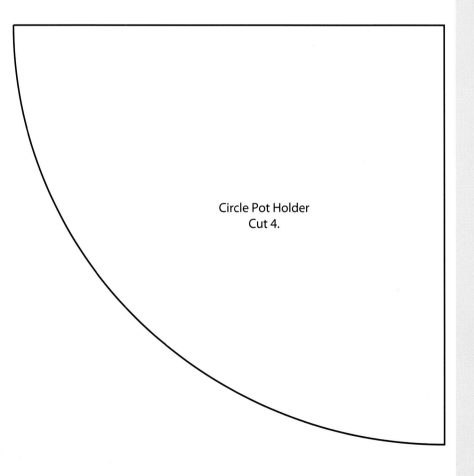

Circle Pot Holder
Cut 4.

Makes 1 pot holder.

FABRIC FOR FRONT:
4 prints, each cut 6″ × 6″

FABRIC FOR BACK: 10″ × 10″

BINDING: 1 fat quarter

COTTON BATTING: 9″ × 9″

INSUL-FLEECE (BY C&T PUBLISHING): 9″ × 9″

SCALLOPED PLACEMATS

Designed and made by Sweetwater

FINISHED PLACEMAT:
approximately 14½″ × 14½″

To achieve a unified look that isn't too "matchy," use a different print for the scalloped edge on each placemat while keeping the main fabric the same. It will make your table setting more interesting—and more colorful.

7. occurring
truth; a simple
nditional: a fran
a simple soldie

single.   7. occurring or considered alone;
simple truth; a simple fact.   8. free of deceit
; unconditional: a frank, simple answer.   9.
inary: a simple soldier.   10. not grand or

refreshing, as air.   12. denoting a young wine
esp. a white or rosé, that is clean, crisp, and
uncomplicated.   13. Meteorology. (of wind
moderately strong or brisk.   14. inexperienced

INSTRUCTIONS

The instructions are for 1 placemat. The pattern is at the left; a ¼" seam allowance is included.

1. Cut 2 pieces 15" × 13" of the main fabric.

2. Use the pattern to cut 2 pieces of the scallop trim fabric.

3. With the right sides together, sew a scallop trim piece to each main fabric piece along a 15" side.

4. Press the seams to one side.

5. Cut a piece of batting 17" × 17". With the right sides together, center the front and the back of the placemat over the cotton batting.

6. Sew all the layers together all around the edges, leaving a 3" opening at the edge opposite the scallop trim.

7. Trim away the excess batting.

8. Clip the curves and trim the corners.

9. Turn the placemat right side out through the opening. Slipstitch the opening closed.

10. Machine quilt the placemat in a crosshatch pattern, placing the stitching lines 2" apart.

Scalloped Placemats
Cut 2 for each placemat.

Enlarge 200%.

what you
need

Makes 4 placemats.

MAIN FABRIC: 1⅜ yards

FABRIC FOR SCALLOP TRIM:
4 prints, each cut
3" × width of fabric

COTTON BATTING: 1⅛ yards

Designed and made by Sweetwater

EMBELLISHED
KITCHEN TOWELS

Turn a plain white kitchen towel into something special with just a little fabric and trickrack.

INSTRUCTIONS

1. Turn the trim fabric under ¼″ along each long edge and press in place.

2. Place the trim fabric over the front of the towel, positioning the top of the fabric 4″ from the bottom edge of the towel.

3. Tuck the rickrack under the trim fabric so that only half of it shows at the bottom of the fabric and pin in place.

4. Fold the fabric and rickrack under at the side edges to match the sides of the towel.

5. Topstitch close to the edges of the trim fabric.

the
OFFICE

Whether you work at home or simply need a place to write letters and pay bills, a home office doesn't have to look boring.

Shop for items that are both stylish and functional. Decorate small jars to store paper clips, staples, and thumbtacks. Our Birthday Board not only keeps you organized but also looks fantastic framed and hung on an office wall. Labels are a great way to personalize your space. Try our fabric version, or simply write on paper tags and dress them up with ribbon.

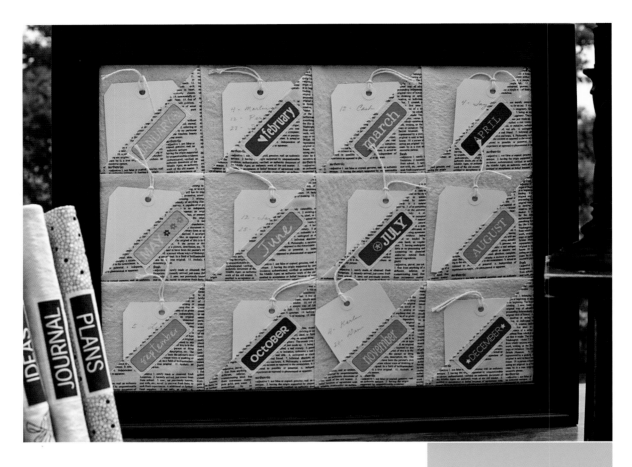

BIRTHDAY BOARD

Designed and made by Sweetwater

FINISHED BOARD: 18" × 14"
(opening in frame)

Never forget another birthday! On this wallhanging, simply write each birthday on the corresponding month's tag. If you are super organized, start each year by making or purchasing cards for the entire year. Address them and store them by month on the Birthday Board, and all you have to do is write in them and drop them in the mail!

INSTRUCTIONS

A ¼" seam allowance is included.

Background and Pockets

1. Cut 12 squares 5" × 5" from the canvas duck cloth for the background.

2. Cut 12 squares 5" × 5" from the pocket fabric.

3. Fold the pocket squares in half diagonally, wrong sides together.

4. To make the fabric labels using a computer and iron-on inkjet-printable fabric, follow the instructions of the printable-fabric manufacturer to make 12 labels each measuring 1" × 3".

5. Peel off the paper backing, if any, from the labels and iron a label to each pocket, with the label placed close to the folded edge.

6. Stitch close around the edges of the labels.

7. Place the pockets over the canvas squares, matching the raw edges on both the bottoms and the right sides.

8. Baste the raw edges of the pocket squares to the canvas squares.

9. Arrange the squares by month. With the right sides together, sew them together by first sewing 4 squares in a row. Press. Repeat this until you have 3 rows of 4 squares.

10. Sew the 3 rows together. Press.

11. Check that the piece fits your frame opening and trim it to size if required. Zigzag the outer edges to keep them from raveling.

Frame

1. Trace the opening edges on the frame back. To secure the fabric to the frame back, place double-stick carpet tape along the traced edges on the back.

2. Place the fabric over the tape and then insert it into the frame.

Tags

1. Punch holes in the tops of the manila tags, if necessary.

2. Tie 6" pieces of cotton string through the holes in the tags.

3. Record each birthday on the tag for the appropriate month, and place the tag in that month's pocket.

what you need

FABRIC FOR BACKGROUND:
½ yard canvas duck cloth

FABRIC FOR POCKETS: ½ yard

MONTHLY IRON-ON FABRIC LABELS
(see Resources, page 140)
or 1 sheet iron-on inkjet-printable fabric

12 MANILA SHEETS OR
TAGS, each cut 3" × 4"

COTTON STRING

FRAME with 18" × 14" opening
(Choose a frame that has a back.)

DOUBLE-STICK CARPET TAPE

Helpful Hint

You can buy iron-on labels from Sweetwater that can be custom printed with any words you choose. As an alternative to these, you can use inkjet-printable fabric with iron-on adhesive on the back.

OFFICE LAMP

Designed and made by Sweetwater

This lampshade was created with an inexpensive purchased shade and some fabric, using the decoupage technique. If you haven't used this technique before, it is fun and easy. The decoupage medium acts as glue but dries clear. You can't mess it up! We used one fabric for the whole shade; for another look, try using a different print for each section of the shade.

INSTRUCTIONS

1. Place a piece of paper over a section of the lamp shade and trace the shape. If the shade doesn't have seamed sections but is a continuous piece of fabric, measure the dimensions of a section of the wire frame with a tape measure and draw the shape on paper.

2. Use the traced pattern to cut fabric for each section.

3. Using a sponge brush, apply decoupage medium to the back of each piece of fabric.

4. Place each piece of fabric on a section of the lamp and smooth the fabric with your fingers.

5. Cut strips of fabric 1″ × the length of the shade for each seam on the shade.

6. Fold under the raw edges of each strip toward the center and press.

7. Apply decoupage medium to the seams of the shade and place the strips over the seams. Smooth the fabric with your fingers.

8. Cut 2 strips of fabric 1″ × the circumference of the shade at the top and bottom.

9. Repeat Steps 6 and 7, except apply the strips from Step 8 around the top and bottom of the shade instead of over the seams.

10. Brush several thin coats of decoupage medium over the entire surface of the lamp shade. The decoupage will dry clear.

what you need

PURCHASED CLOTH LAMP SHADE with vertical wired sections, any size

PRINTED FABRIC (the amount depends on the size of the shade)

SPONGE BRUSH

DECOUPAGE MEDIUM such as Mod Podge (by Plaid; available at craft supply stores)

NOTEPAD COVER

FINISHED NOTEPAD COVER:
5½″ wide × 9″ high × 1″ deep
when folded

Designed and made by Sweetwater

Remember those old book covers you were required to slip on your junior high science books? Try this updated version—a little more stylish and a lot more fun. Two inside pockets hold two standard 5″ × 8″ notepads; a magnetic closure keeps them secure.

INSTRUCTIONS

The pattern is on page 46; a ¼" seam allowance is included.

Outside and Batting

1. Cut 1 piece 12½" × 9½" from the outside fabric.

2. With the right side up, center the outside piece over the cotton batting.

3. Baste the outside fabric and the cotton batting together, close to the raw edge.

4. Trim away the excess batting and treat the two pieces as one.

Label

1. To make the fabric labels using a computer and iron-on inkjet-printable fabric, follow the instructions of the printable-fabric manufacturer to make a label measuring 1" × 3".

2. Peel off the paper backing (if there is one) from the label and iron it to the center of the outside piece with the label positioned vertically.

3. Stitch close around the edge of the label.

Lining and Pockets

1. Cut 1 piece 12½" × 9½" from the lining fabric.

2. Cut 1 pocket piece 12½" × 12" from the pocket fabric.

3. Fold the pocket piece in half with the wrong sides together, matching the 12½" sides. Press.

4. Place the folded pocket piece over the lining piece, matching the raw edges at the sides and bottom.

5. Baste the pocket to the lining close to the raw edges.

6. Stitch down the center of the pocket to form 2 pockets, as shown.

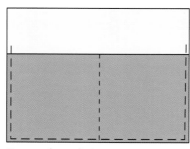

Baste pocket to lining.

Closure Tab

1. Use the pattern to cut 2 pieces for the tab. Cut a piece of batting 3½" × 5".

2. With right side up, center 1 tab piece over the cotton batting.

3. Baste the fabric and batting together, close to the raw edge. Trim away the excess batting. This will be the underside of the tab.

4. Apply 1 part of the magnetic closure to the underside of the tab according to the manufacturer's directions. Position the magnet closure in the center and ¾" in from the edge.

5. With the right sides together, place the remaining tab piece over the underside piece. Sew the pieces together, leaving the straight side open.

6. Trim the seam allowance to ⅛".

7. Turn the closure tab right side out and press.

8. Topstitch close to the edge.

9. Center the tab along the left 9½" edge of the outside piece, with the underside facing up. Baste in place.

10. Apply the second part of the magnet closure to the opposite side on the outside cover, placing the closure in the center and 1" in from the edge.

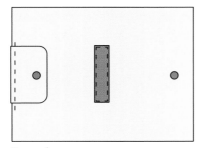

Baste tab to cover.

Finishing

1. With the right sides together, pin the lining to the outside.

2. Trim all the corners to make them rounded.

3. Sew the lining and the outside cover together all around the edge, leaving a 3" opening at the bottom.

4. Turn the piece right side out through the opening and press.

5. Topstitch close to the edge around the entire cover. This will secure the opening closed.

6. Insert a notepad into each pocket.

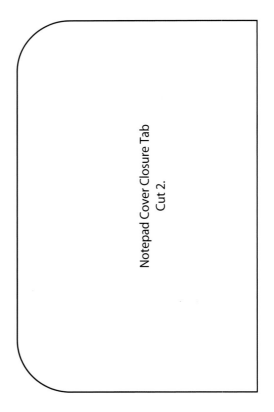

Notepad Cover Closure Tab
Cut 2.

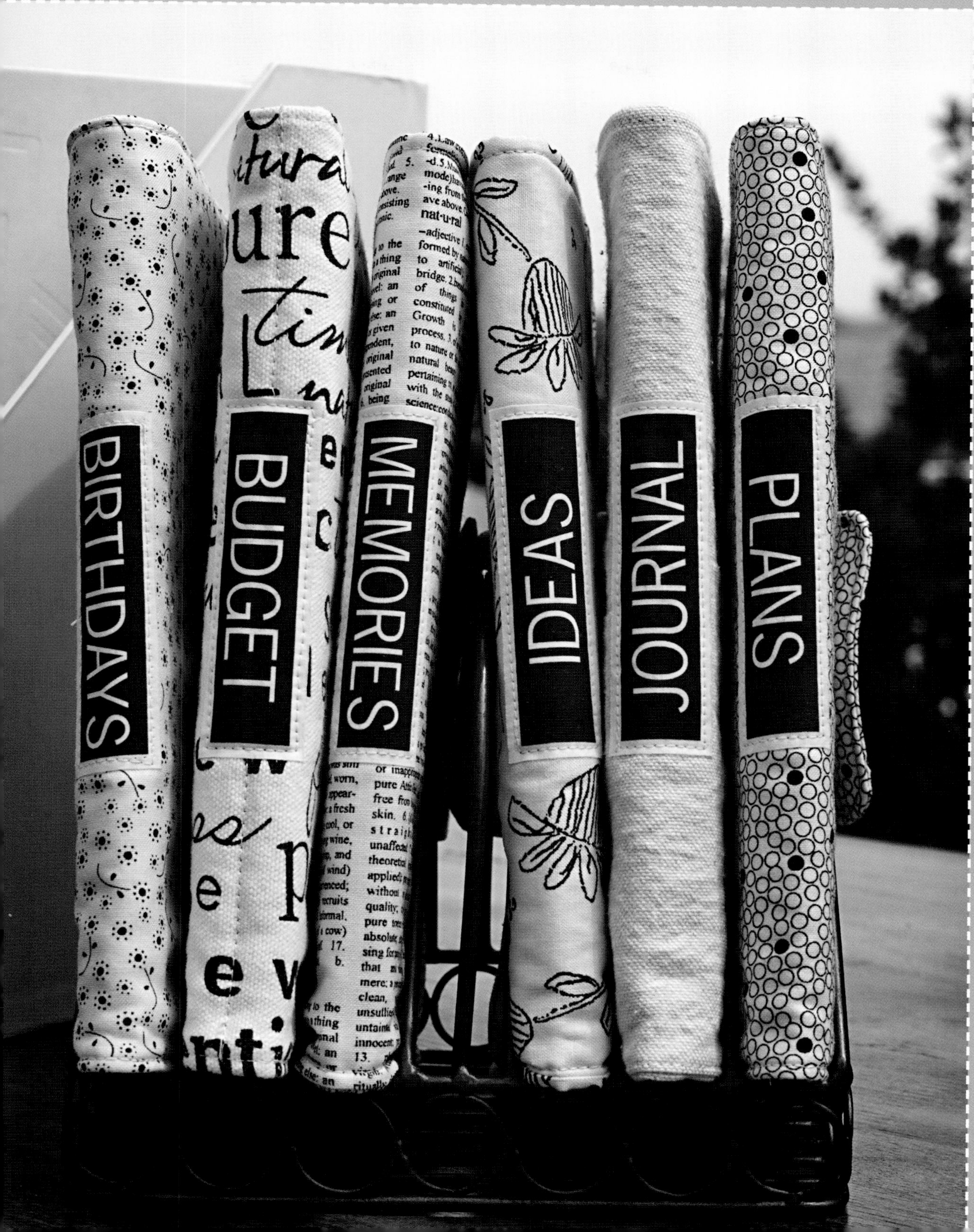
BIRTHDAYS
BUDGET
MEMORIES
IDEAS
JOURNAL
PLANS

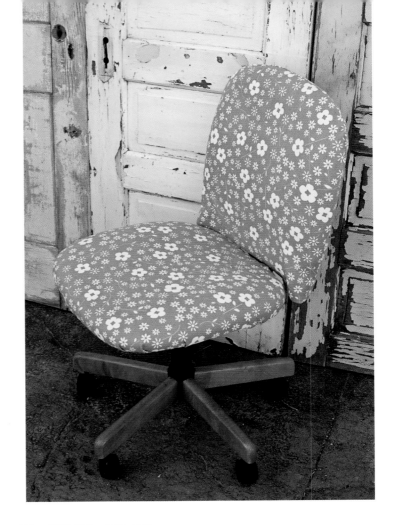

COVERED OFFICE
CHAIR *Designed and made by Sweetwater*

Freshen up your everyday work chair with this quick and easy "slipcover." The technique for making this cover will work for any size of chair back and seat.

INSTRUCTIONS

A ¼″ seam allowance is included.

1. Place the fabric over the seat of the chair with enough fabric to be tacked to the underside.

2. Using a staple gun, staple the fabric in place. Pleat it with your fingers as you work to get a snug, smooth fit.

3. Lay the chair on its back and trace the back shape on 2 layers of fabric with the right sides together, adding ½″ at the bottom edge for a hem.

4. Stitch on the traced line, leaving the bottom edge open.

5. Trim the seam allowance to ¼″ and turn the piece right side out. Press.

6. Hem the bottom opening by turning under ¼″ twice and topstitching. Slip the cover over the back of the chair.

CANVAS DUCK CLOTH or other heavyweight fabric (depending on the size of the chair), approximately 2 yards 52″-wide

STAPLE GUN

OFFICE ACCESSORIES

Create stylish accessories by adding your own hand-made touches to everyday purchased and reused items.

Dress up a purchased chalkboard with fresh white paint on the frame and stenciled words on the board. You could also build one like ours using materials from your local hardware store, lumberyard, or home improvement store. We had a piece of Masonite cut at the lumberyard, and we painted it with chalkboard paint. The frame is made of 1″ × 3″ boards, attached with Liquid Nails adhesive and 1″ screws. We inserted a cotton rope hanger through holes drilled into the top of the frame and stenciled the word "Renew" using white craft paint.

To make this pencil holder, we recycled a common super-market drink carrier by covering it with fusible-backed fabric. We simply traced the shape of the sides, ends, and handle on the fabric, cut it out, and ironed it to the carrier. The edges are left raw, trimmed even with the carrier edges.

the
MASTER SUITE

It has been said that we spend half our lives asleep. If this is true, our bedrooms should truly be our sanctuaries. Your bedroom can be the most personal space in your home. Surround yourself with things you love— photos, candles, and, of course, quilts. Your bed should always be a welcome space, a place where you want to be. Fill it with your favorite colors, cozy blankets, and beautiful pillows.

MASTER SUITE
QUILT

Designed and made by Sweetwater
and machine quilted by Brian Clements

FINISHED QUILT: 80½″ × 93½″
FINISHED BLOCK: 9″ × 9″

Although this queen-size quilt isn't one you will complete in an afternoon, it truly is simple to make, and it's so satisfying to use and admire when it's all finished.

INSTRUCTIONS

A ¼" seam allowance is included.

Blocks

1. Cut 4 pieces 5" × 4" from a 10" × 10" print square.

2. Cut 4 pieces 5" × 1½" from a print strip.

3. With right sides together, sew a 5" × 1½" piece to each 5" × 4" piece along the 5" side. Press the seams to one side.

Make 4.

4. Sew the 4 pieces together as shown to make 1 block 9½" × 9½" unfinished.

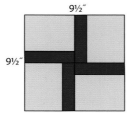

Make 30.

5. Repeat Steps 1–4 to make a total of 30 blocks.

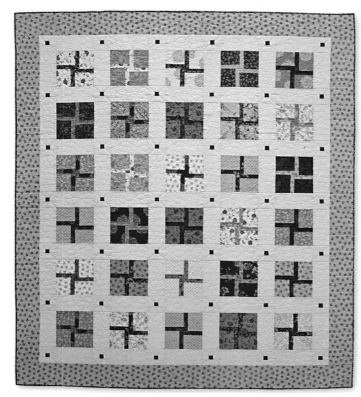

what you
need

FABRIC FOR BLOCKS:

    30 different prints, each cut 10" × 10", or 10" × 10" precut pack

    30 different prints, each cut 1½" × width of fabric, or 1½"-wide strip bundle

FABRIC FOR SASHING CORNERSTONES:

    ⅛ yard solid red fabric

    1 yard solid cream fabric

FABRIC FOR SASHING:
2½ yards solid cream fabric

FABRIC FOR BORDERS: 1¾ yards

BINDING: ¾ yard

BACKING FABRIC: 88" × 101"

BATTING: 88" × 101"

Sashing Cornerstones

1. Cut 2 strips 1½″ × the width of the fabric from the red sashing cornerstone fabric. Subcut the strips into 42 squares 1½″ × 1½″.

2. Cut 4 strips 2″ × the width of the fabric from the cream sashing cornerstone fabric. Subcut the strips into 84 pieces 2″ × 1½″.

3. Sew 2 pieces of cream fabric to opposite sides of a red square.

4. Cut 11 strips 2″ × the width of the fabric from the cream fabric. Subcut the strips into 84 pieces 2″ × 4½″.

5. Sew the 2″ × 4½″ pieces of cream fabric to the sides of the red square unit as shown.

6. Repeat Steps 1–5 to make a total of 42 sashing cornerstones 4½″ × 4½″ (unfinished).

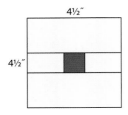

Make 42.

Sashing

1. Cut 18 strips 4½″ × the width of the fabric from the sashing fabric. Subcut the 18 strips into 71 pieces 4½″ × 9½″.

2. Sew sashing pieces between the blocks and at both ends to make a row with 5 blocks. Press toward the sashing.

3. Repeat Step 2 with the remaining blocks to make a total of 6 rows.

4. Sew sashing corners between the sashing pieces and at both ends to make a strip with 6 sashing corners. Press toward the sashing.

5. Repeat Step 4 with the remaining sashing corners to make a total of 7 strips.

6. Referring to the quilt assembly diagram (page 57), sew the strips in between the rows and at both ends, pressing toward the sashing rows as you go along.

Borders

1. Cut 9 strips 6″ × the width of the fabric.

2. Refer to Borders (page 136) to sew the strips to the sides, top, and bottom of the quilt.

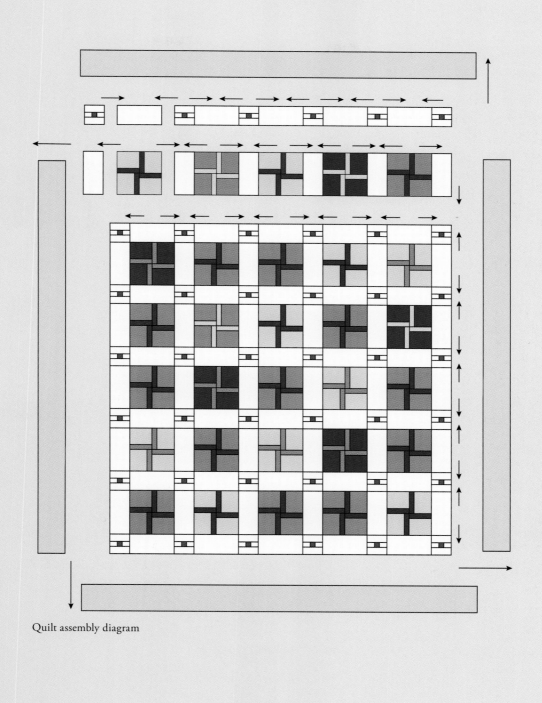

Quilt assembly diagram

Finishing

For the binding, cut 10 strips 2¼″ × the width of the fabric; sew together using diagonal seams to make 1 long strip.

Refer to Basic Techniques (page 135) to layer, quilt, and bind the quilt. Quilt your quilt top as desired. Our quilt features an allover leaf and vine design.

LARGE TIE PILLOW

Designed and made by Sweetwater

FINISHED PILLOW: 42" × 16"

We have seen these large covered body pillows in our favorite home stores, but they are always very expensive. We saved about $50 by purchasing an inexpensive body pillow at a discount store and covering it with some of our favorite fabric.

INSTRUCTIONS

A ¼″ seam allowance is included.

1. Open an end of the body pillow and reduce the length to measure the width of your fabric. You may need to remove some of the stuffing.

2. Slipstitch the opening closed.

3. With the right sides together, fold the pillow cover fabric in half, matching the long sides.

4. Cut the twill tape into 4 pieces 18″ long and fold each piece in half crosswise.

5. Sandwich the twill tape pieces between the folded fabric layers, positioning the tape 6″ from each long edge.

6. Pin and sew around the sides and bottom, leaving an 18″ opening in the center.

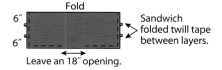

7. Turn the pillow cover right side out and press.

8. Insert the body pillow into the pillow cover and slipstitch the opening closed.

9. Tie the twill tape into bows.

what you ***need***

RED STRIPED PILLOW
COVER FABRIC: 1 yard

½″-WIDE TWILL TAPE: 2 yards

1 BODY-SIZE PILLOW

Helpful Hint

We reduced the length of the body-size pillow because it was longer than the width of our fabric, and we wanted to avoid piecing the cover.

MAKE LIFE SWEET PILLOW

Designed and made by Sweetwater

We love the saying "Make Life Sweet," but you can choose anything you wish. Try the words "Sweet Dreams" using the embroidery pattern (page 121). For a more personalized pillow, embroider a name instead of a phrase.

INSTRUCTIONS

The embroidery pattern is below; a ¼″ seam allowance is included.

To create the words for the embroidery, you can use the pattern provided or print the words using a computer. Try using a handwriting font; many fonts are readily available for personal use on free font sites on the Internet. Make sure your phrase is no longer than 20″. You can also use your own handwriting for the pattern; use lined notebook paper to keep the writing even.

1. Cut 2 pieces 22″ × 12″ of the linen fabric.

2. Trace the words "Make Life Sweet" from the pattern to make a template for the embroidery. Enlarge and copy the words 150% to make the finished template. On 1 piece of linen, center the finished template and trace the words with a pencil. (You may need to use a lightbox or hold the linen up to a window.)

3. With 3 strands of embroidery floss, embroider the words using a backstitch.

4. With the right sides together, sew the pillow front to the back, leaving a 4″ opening at the bottom.

5. Trim the corners, turn the pillow cover right side out, and press.

6. Stuff the pillow and hand sew the opening closed.

make Life sweet

Enlarge 150%.

DRAWSTRING
BAG *Designed and made by Sweetwater*

FINISHED BAG: approximately
6″ diameter × 10¾″ high

This bag, with its four handy outer pockets, is great for storing personal toiletries such as cotton swabs, lotion, and soap. Keep it packed with the essentials, and you're all set for overnight trips.

INSTRUCTIONS

The pattern is on page 67; a ¼″ seam allowance is included.

Bag Top

1. Cut 2 pieces 10″ × 8″ from the bag top fabric.

2. With the right sides together, sew the 2 pieces together along the 8″ sides, leaving a 1″ opening on each side, 2¾″ down from the top. Backstitch at each end of the 1″ openings.

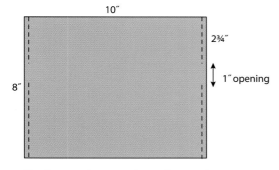

Sew bag top pieces together to form a tube.

3. Fold the top edge of the tube ¼″ to the wrong side and press.

4. Fold the edge again 1¾″ to the wrong side and press.

5. Topstitch close to the first folded edge and then again 1″ from the first stitching to form the casing for the ties.

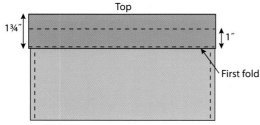

Make the casing.

what you need

FABRIC FOR BAG TOP: ⅓ yard

FABRIC FOR BAG SIDES, POCKETS, AND BOTTOM: ⅓ yard canvas duck cloth

FABRIC FOR DRAWSTRING: 6″ × width of fabric

Bag Sides, Pockets, and Bottom

1. Cut 2 pieces 10″ × 6″ from the canvas duck cloth for the sides.

2. Using the pattern, cut the bottom piece from the canvas duck cloth.

3. Cut 2 pieces 10″ × 5″ from the canvas duck cloth for the pockets.

4. Fold a 10″ edge 1/4″ to the wrong side on the pocket pieces and press.

5. Fold again ¼″ to the wrong side and press. Topstitch close to the first folded edge.

6. Place the pocket pieces over the side pieces, matching the raw edges along the lower edges.

7. Baste the pieces together close to the edges.

8. Stitch down the center of each pocket to make a pocket on each side.

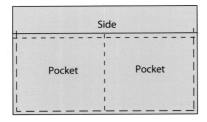

Side/pocket piece

9. With the right sides together, sew the 2 side/pocket pieces together along the 6″ sides. Press.

10. With the right sides together, sew the bag side/pockets to the bottom circle. Zigzag the seams to keep them from raveling.

11. With the right sides together, sew the bag top and side/pocket/bottom section together.

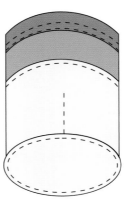

Sew bag top to side/pocket/bottom section.

12. Turn the bag right side out and press the seam to one side.

13. Push the top section down into the bottom section, creating a fold along the top seamline.

14. Topstitch ¼″ from the seamline.

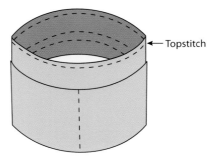

Topstitch ¼″ from seamline.

Drawstrings

1. Cut 2 strips 2″ × 30″ of the drawstring fabric.

2. With the *wrong* sides together, fold the long edges of each strip to the center and press.

3. Fold the strips lengthwise again, matching the folded edges. Topstitch close to both long edges.

4. Attach a safety pin to an end and push it through 1 of the casing openings. Bring the strip out through the same opening.

5. Insert the other strip through the other casing opening and bring it out through the same opening.

6. Trim the ends at a diagonal and tie them together in a knot. Pull the drawstrings to close the bag.

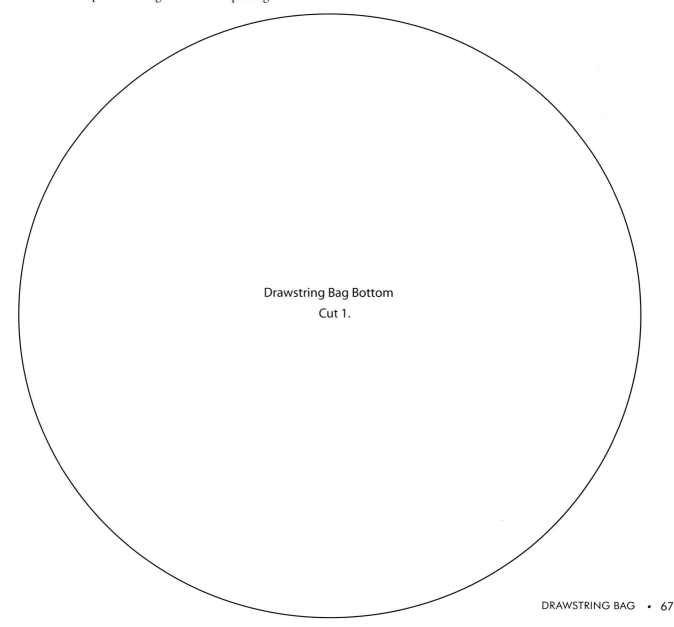

Drawstring Bag Bottom
Cut 1.

TRAY LINER

Designed and made by Sweetwater

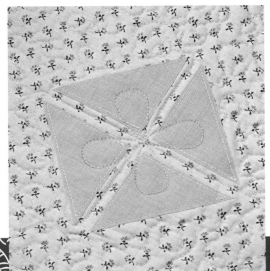

We used a combination of piecing and raw-edge fused appliqué to create this small quilted liner. It provides a nice touch on a purchased tray and is removable for easy laundering.

INSTRUCTIONS

A ¼″ seam allowance is included.

Measure the inside of the bottom of the tray and cut the background fabric the same size.

Center Appliqué

1. Draw a 4″ square onto the paper side of the fusible web.

2. Iron the fusible web to the wrong side of the coordinating fabric, following the manufacturer's instructions.

3. Cut the square out on the drawn line.

4. Cut the square in half diagonally and then diagonally again to make 4 triangles.

5. Peel off the paper backing and iron the triangles to the center of the background fabric, placing them ¼″ apart. Refer to the diagram (below).

6. Topstitch close to the edges of the triangles.

Corners

1. Cut 2 squares 5″ × 5″ from the coordinating fabric.

2. Cut the squares in half diagonally to make 4 triangles.

3. Turn the fabric under ¼″ along the diagonal edges and press.

4. Place a triangle at each corner of the main fabric, matching the corners.

5. Cut a piece of rickrack for each corner triangle, tuck it halfway under the turned-under edge, and topstitch it in place through all the layers.

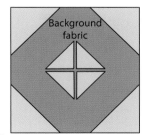

Background fabric

Finishing

Cut 2 or 3 strips (depending on the size of the tray liner) 2¼″ × the width of the fabric from the binding fabric.

Refer to Basic Techniques (page 135) to layer, quilt, and bind the tray liner. On our tray liner, the center is stipple quilted, and there is a flower pattern quilted in the corner triangles.

Quantities may vary depending on the actual size of the tray.

TRAY: any size (A square tray works best for this project; our sample is about 13″ × 13″.)

FABRIC FOR BACKGROUND: ½ yard

FABRIC TO COORDINATE:
1 fat quarter

PAPER-BACKED FUSIBLE WEB: ¼ yard

½″-WIDE RICKRACK: 1 yard

BATTING: slightly larger than tray (We used 17″ × 17″ for our sample.)

BACKING FABRIC: ½ yard

BINDING: ¼ yard

EMBELLISHED BATH TOWELS

Designed and made by Sweetwater

Don't just save these pretty towels for guests. Treat yourself to big, fluffy towels every day.

INSTRUCTIONS

Makes 1 towel.

1. Turn the edge of the strip under ¼″ along each long side and press.

2. Position the fabric strip over the woven border of the towel and pin in place.

3. Tuck the fabric strip under at the ends at the side edges to match the sides of the towel.

4. Topstitch along the folded edges of the fabric.

what you need

TOWELS: any size—bath towels, hand towels, or washcloths

FABRIC FOR EACH TOWEL: 1¾″ × width of towel, plus additional 1″

the LAUNDRY ROOM

Whether it's in a closet or its own dedicated room, the laundry area may be the busiest space in your home. Make yours functional and beautiful with coordinating hampers and storage containers. You may even look forward to laundry day!

TIED HAMPER

Designed and made by Sweetwater

This hamper may make doing laundry just a touch more joyful. Replace the bag that comes on the purchased wood frame with fabric in a color that makes you happy, and you'll cease to dread this never-ending chore.

INSTRUCTIONS

A ¼″ seam allowance is included.

Outside and Lining

1. Cut 1 piece 13½″ × 13½″ from each of the outside fabric and the lining fabric for the bottom.

2. Cut 4 pieces 13½″ × 23″ from each of the outside fabric and the lining fabric for the sides.

3. With the right sides together, sew the 4 outside fabric sides together along the 23″ sides.

4. With the right sides together, sew the sides to the outside fabric bottom piece, matching the corners of the bottom with the side seams.

5. Turn this piece right side out.

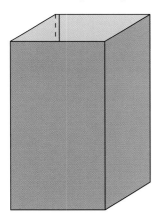

Turn outside fabric piece right side out.

6. Repeat Steps 3–5 for the lining pieces, except do not turn the lining piece right side out after sewing.

7. Insert the lining into the outside piece, with the wrong sides together and matching the top raw edges.

8. Baste the lining to the outside, close to the top raw edges.

Twill Tape Ties

1. Cut the twill tape into 6 pieces 18″ long and fold each piece in half crosswise.

2. Pin 3 folded pieces of twill tape to the top edge of 1 side of the hamper, on the inside, next to the lining and matching the folds with the raw edges. Position 2 of the ties next to the corner seams and 1 in the center.

3. Pin the other 3 ties in the same manner on the opposite side.

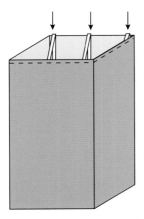

Pin folded twill tape to inside top edge.

Facing

1. Cut 4 pieces 13½″ × 3″ from the facing fabric.

2. With the right sides together, sew the 4 pieces together along the 3″ sides.

3. Turn the fabric under ¼″ along 1 edge and press.

4. With the right sides together, insert the facing into the hamper against the lining, matching the raw edge of the facing to the raw edges of the hamper, with the ties sandwiched in between. Sew together and press the seam toward the facing.

5. Turn the facing to the outside of the hamper and press again.

6. Topstitch the facing to the outside along the turned-under edge of the facing.

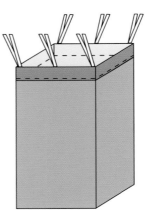

Press facing to outside and topstitch.

7. Tie the twill tape to the wooden frame of the hamper.

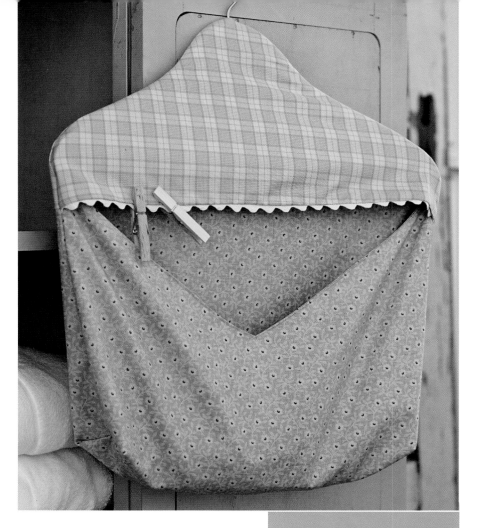

CLOTHESPIN
BAG

Designed and made by Sweetwater

FINISHED BAG: approximately 17" wide × 17" high × 3" deep

Make sure to use a wooden hanger when making this project. It will be sturdier than a wire hanger, so your bag will hold more clothespins.

INSTRUCTIONS

A ¼″ seam allowance is included.

Front Top Section

1. Place the hanger on 2 layers of front top section fabric folded with the *wrong* sides together.

2. Trace around the hanger, adding 2″ to the length and ¼″ to the top curved line as shown. Cut out the traced shape.

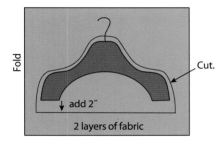

Trace around hanger.

3. Place a length of rickrack on the right side of a top piece, along the lower straight edge. Stitch along the center of the rickrack.

4. With the right sides together, sew the other top piece to the piece with the rickrack along the straight edge only, using the stitching on the rickrack as a guide.

5. Turn the pieces right side out and press.

6. Baste the top curved raw edges together and treat as 1 piece.

what you need

PURCHASED WOOD HANGER, approximately 17″ wide

FABRIC FOR FRONT TOP SECTION: ¼ yard

FABRIC FOR FRONT BOTTOM SECTION AND BACK: 1⅛ yards

½″-WIDE RICKRACK: ⅔ yard

Back

1. Place the front top section on 2 layers of back fabric folded with the *wrong* sides together.

2. Trace around the front top section, adding 12″ at the bottom as shown. Cut out the traced shape.

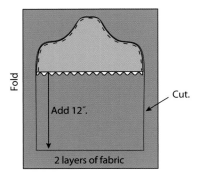

Trace around front top section and add 12″.

3. Baste the back fabric layers together around the raw edges and treat as 1 piece.

Front Bottom Section

1. Cut 2 pieces 13½″ × the width of the back piece from the front bottom fabric.

2. Fold the 2 pieces in half, matching the 13½″ sides.

3. Mark a point on the fold 5½″ down from the top edge. Draw a line from the marked point to the top outside corner as shown.

4. Cut through all the layers, making a V for the front opening.

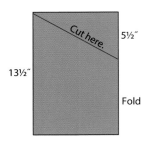

Mark a V in 2 folded layers.

5. With the right sides together, sew the 2 pieces together along the V edge.

6. Clip the V and turn the piece right side out. Press.

7. Topstitch close to the seam.

8. Baste the raw edges together and treat as 1 piece.

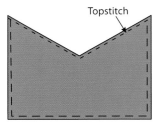

Front bottom section

Finishing

1. With the right sides together, layer the top front section over the back. Then layer the front bottom section on top, with the right side facing down.

2. Sew all around the pieces, leaving a ½″ opening at the top for the hanger hook to slip through.

Sew all around, leaving ½″ opening at top.

3. To construct a flat bottom, match the side and bottom seams together with right sides facing and sew across, 2″ from each corner.

Sew across, 2″ from corners.

4. Turn the cover right side out and press.

5. Insert the hanger at the top.

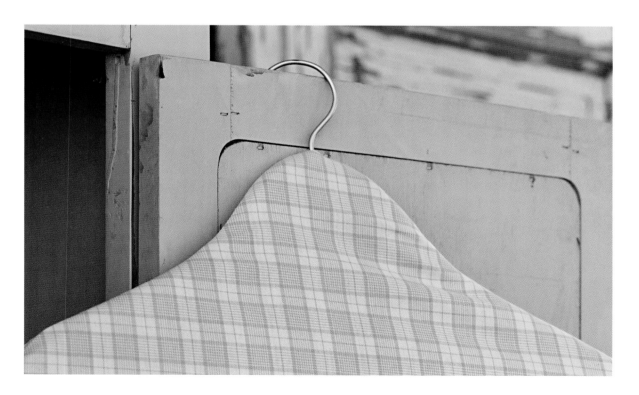

ORGANIZING JAR LABELS

Designed and made by Sweetwater

Glass jars filled with laundry supplies and equipped with these attractive custom labels not only keep you organized but also look much cuter than open laundry soap boxes and containers of dryer sheets.

INSTRUCTIONS

A ¼″ seam allowance is included. Instructions are for 1 label.

Background

1. Cut 1 piece of canvas 4″ × 3″ and 1 piece 5″ × 4″.

2. Cut 1 piece of batting 5″ × 4″.

3. Layer the 3 pieces with the batting in the middle, the large rectangle on the bottom right side down, and the small rectangle on the top right side up.

4. Topstitch the layers together close to the raw edge of the top piece of canvas.

5. Trim away the excess batting and fabric from the bottom piece of canvas.

Binding

Refer to Double-Fold Straight-Grain Binding (page 137) to cut and sew on the binding.

Labels

1. To make the fabric labels using a computer and iron-on inkjet-printable fabric, follow the instructions of the printable-fabric manufacturer to make labels measuring 2¾″ × 1¾″.

2. Peel off the paper backing (if there is one) from the label and iron it to the center of the canvas background.

3. Stitch close around the edge of the label.

Ribbon Ties

1. Cut a piece of ribbon 18″ long and fold it in half crosswise.

2. Place the folded edge just below the binding on the back of the canvas.

3. Stitch across the ribbon, close to the binding, to secure it in place.

4. Use the ribbon tie to hang the label on the jar.

what you need

Makes 6 labels.

FABRIC FOR BACKGROUND:
¼ yard canvas fabric

BINDING: 6 prints, 2¼″ × width of fabric (1 print for each label)

6 IRON-ON FABRIC LABELS (see Resources, page 140) or 1 sheet iron-on inkjet-printable fabric

COTTON BATTING: 6″ × 30″

½″-WIDE RIBBON FOR TIES: 3 yards

Helpful Hint

You can buy iron-on labels from Sweetwater that can be custom printed with any words you choose. As an alternative to these, you can use inkjet-printable fabric with iron-on adhesive on the back.

the FAMILY ROOM

The family room or game room should always be a happy place. Kids will love the bright colors in this quilt, and the large floor cushions will keep them comfortable while playing their favorite game on a hand-made "checkerboard."

FAMILY ROOM
QUILT

Designed and made by Sweetwater
and machine quilted by Brian Clements

FINISHED QUILT: 52½" × 59½"
FINISHED BLOCK: 9½" × 4½"

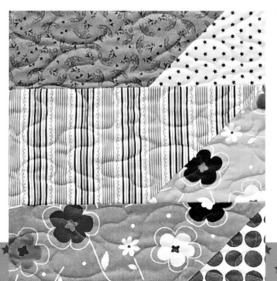

This quilt will make any room brighter. We love these happy, vibrant colors, especially against a neutral background.

INSTRUCTIONS

A ¼" seam allowance is included.

Blocks

Makes 40 blocks.

1. Cut the 40 squares in half to measure 10″ × 5″.

2. Cut 40 of the 10″ × 5″ pieces in half to measure 5″ × 5″.

3. Mark 40 of the 5″ × 5″ squares diagonally with a pencil on the wrong side.

FABRIC FOR BLOCKS:
40 different prints,
each cut 10″ × 10″, or
10″ × 10″ precut pack

FABRIC FOR MIDDLE BORDER:
fabric left over from 10″ squares

FABRIC FOR INNER AND
OUTER BORDERS: 1¼ yards
solid-color fabric

BINDING: ½ yard

BACKING FABRIC: 60″ × 67″

BATTING: 60″ × 67″

4. Mark the 5″ × 5″ squares again, this time ½″ away from the first line.

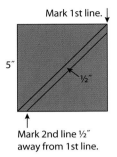

Mark 1st line. ↓

5″

½″

Mark 2nd line ½″ away from 1st line.

Mark 40 squares.

5. With the right sides together, place a marked 5″ × 5″ piece over a 10″ × 5″ piece.

6. Stitch on the marked lines.

7. With a rotary cutter, cut in between the stitching (the solid line in the diagram).

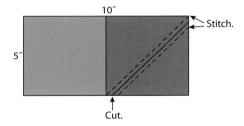

10″

Stitch.

5″

Cut.

Stitch on marked lines.

8. Press the triangle back. The block will measure 10″ × 5″.

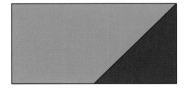

Make 40.

The leftover half-square triangle piece can be used to piece the back of the quilt or can be saved for another project.

Rows

1. With the right sides together, sew 4 blocks together along the 5″ sides to make 1 row. Press, alternating directions in adjoining rows.

2. Repeat with the remaining blocks to make a total of 10 rows. Press.

3. Sew the rows together. Press.

Borders

This quilt has an inner border, a middle border, and an outer border. Refer to Borders (page 136) to sew the strips to the sides, top, and bottom of the quilt. Press the seam allowances of the middle border toward the adjacent borders.

1. Cut 5 strips 2″ × the width of the fabric from the solid-color fabric for the inner border.

2. Cut strips 1½″ × 5″ and 1½″ × 2½″ from the remaining 5″ × 5″ squares of printed fabric for the middle border. Randomly sew these pieces together along the 1½″ sides to make strips that fit the sides, top, and bottom of the quilt.

3. Cut 6 pieces 5″ × the width of the fabric from the solid-color fabric for the outer border.

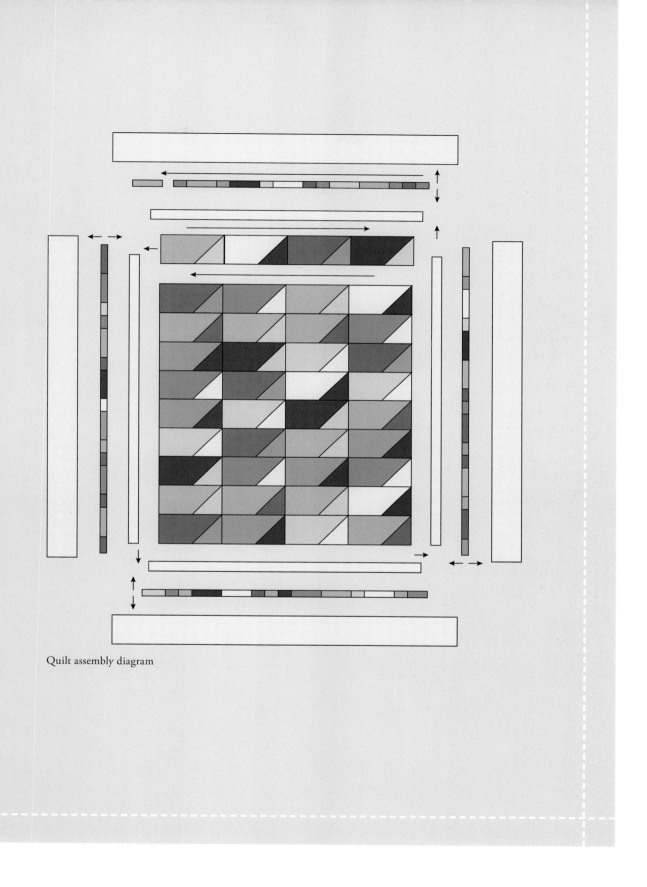

Quilt assembly diagram

Finishing

For the binding, cut 7 strips 2¼″ × the width of the fabric; sew together using diagonal seams to make 1 long strip.

Refer to Basic Techniques (page 135) to layer, quilt, and bind the quilt.

Quilt your quilt top as desired. Our quilt features a design of swirls and circles.

Helpful Hint

The leftover half-square triangles can be pieced in between larger pieces to make the backing or saved for another project.

ROUND FLOOR CUSHION

Designed and made by Sweetwater

FINISHED FLOOR CUSHION:
17½" diameter × 4" high

Make coordinating cushions for each member of your family. Let children choose their favorite colors and fabrics to make them even more special.

INSTRUCTIONS

The pattern is on page 95; a ¼″ seam allowance is included.

Cushion Top and Bottom

1. From the canvas fabric, cut 2 squares 19″ × 19″.

2. With the right sides together, fold each square in half and then in half again.

3. Place the pattern over the folded fabric, matching the straight lines of the pattern with the folds. Trace around the curve.

4. Cut along the traced curve to make 2 circles 18″ in diameter.

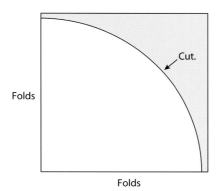

Piping

1. Cut bias strips 1¼″ wide and piece them together diagonally to make 2 strips that measure 60″ long.

Refer to Continuous Bias Binding (page 138) for an alternate method to make the bias strips.

2. To make a piece of piping, cut 1 end of the bias strip at a 45° angle. Fold the end under ½″ and press.

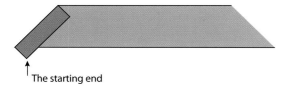

Fold starting end under ½″ and press.

3. With the wrong sides together, fold the strip in half lengthwise.

MAIN FABRIC: 1 yard canvas print for cushion top, bottom, and side band

FABRIC FOR PIPING: 1 fat quarter

³⁄₁₆″ COTTON CLOTHESLINE ROPE: 3½ yards

POLYESTER STUFFING

4. Cut a piece of cotton rope 60″ long.

5. Wrap the bias strip around the cotton rope, positioning the end of the rope about 2″ from the folded end of the strip. Match the raw edges. *Pinning makes it easier to sew.*

6. Using a zipper foot, position the needle of the sewing machine next to the rope and start stitching, leaving the first 2″ open as shown. Stitch to the other end of the bias strip. Trim the seam allowance to ¼″ if necessary.

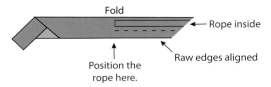

Position rope 2″ from starting end.

7. Repeat Steps 2–6 for the second piece of piping.

8. Beginning at the folded-in end of the piping, position a piece of the piping on the right side of a circle piece, matching the raw edges.

9. Sew the piping to the circle piece directly over the previous row of stitching on the piping.

10. As you approach the starting point, slip the end of the piping into the 2″ opening as shown. Butt the ends of the rope together. Trim away excess piping if necessary and finish stitching.

Slip end of piping into 2″ opening.

11. Repeat Steps 8–10 for the remaining circle and piping piece.

Side Band

1. Cut 4½″-wide strips of canvas fabric and piece together as necessary to make 1 strip 4½″ × 57″.

2. With the right sides together, sew the 4½″ ends together.

3. With the right sides together, sew the band to the top and bottom circles. Stitch directly over the piping stitching. Leave a 4″ opening on 1 of the seams. Zigzag the seams to keep them from raveling.

4. Turn the cover right side out.

5. Stuff the cover with polyester stuffing and slipstitch the opening closed.

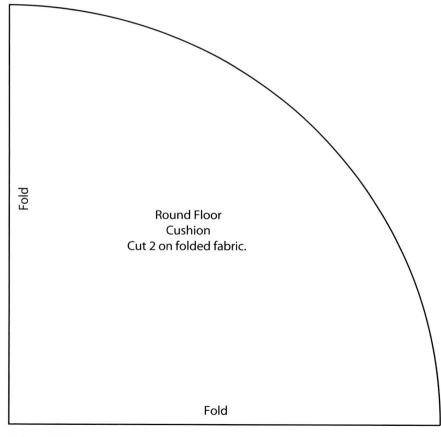

Fold

Round Floor
Cushion
Cut 2 on folded fabric.

Fold

Enlarge 200%.

CHECKERBOARD MAT

Designed and made by Sweetwater

Games are so much fun on a cold winter day. Make checkers even better with this handmade game.

INSTRUCTIONS

A ¼" seam allowance is included. Refer to Basic Techniques (page 135) for further directions.

Mat

1. Cut 32 squares 3½" × 3½" from each print for the mat.

2. With the right sides together, sew 8 squares together to make a row, alternating prints. Press.

3. Make 7 more rows, making sure to alternate the prints. Press, alternating directions in adjacent rows.

4. With the right sides together, sew the rows together to make the mat. Press.

5. Cut 3 strips 2½" × the width of the fabric for the borders.

6. With the right sides together, sew the borders to the top, bottom, and sides of the mat.

7. Layer the backing fabric, batting, and mat together.

8. Using a crosshatch pattern, quilt the mat diagonally across the squares.

9. Trim the excess back and batting.

10. For the binding, cut 4 strips 2¼" wide × the width of the fabric; sew together using diagonal seams to make 1 long strip.

11. Refer to Binding (page 137) to bind the mat.

Checkers

FINISHED CHECKER: 2" × 2"

1. Cut 40 squares 2½" × 2½" from each print.

2. Cut a piece of batting 3" × 3". With the right sides together, center 2 squares over the batting.

3. Sew around the squares through all the layers. Leave a 1½" opening on 1 side.

4. Trim the seam to ⅛" and trim the corners.

5. Turn the square right side out through the opening and press.

6. Topstitch close to the edge of the square and also diagonally from 1 corner to another. This will secure the opening closed.

7. Repeat Steps 2–6 to make a total of 20 checkers from each print.

what you need

FABRIC FOR CHECKERBOARD MAT: 2 prints, ½ yard each

FABRIC FOR BORDER: ⅓ yard

BINDING: ⅓ yard

BACKING FABRIC: 32" × 32"

BATTING: 32" × 32" for mat and 32" × 14" for checkers

FABRIC FOR CHECKERS: 2 prints, ⅓ yard each

the
BABY ROOM

There is nothing sweeter than the smell of a baby, and nothing cuter than all the things that go with a baby. From tiny cotton dresses to fuzzy brown teddy bears, who could resist all the fun? And every baby needs his or her own handmade quilt. It may end up a little ragged, but it will always be loved.

BABY QUILT

*Designed and made by Sweetwater
and machine quilted by Michelle Odle*

This little quilt is sure to be loved by babies and their parents. Diagonal strips, further emphasized by diagonal quilting lines, make a lively design.

INSTRUCTIONS

A ¼″ seam allowance is included.

Blocks

1. Cut 1 piece 6″ × 6″ from each of 2 different 10″ × 10″ prints. Save the scraps for the middle border.

2. From the same print as 1 of the 6″ × 6″ pieces, cut another piece 4″ × 4″.

3. With the right sides together, layer the 6″ × 6″ pieces together.

4. Mark a diagonal line from corner to corner and sew on the marked line.

5. Cut ¼″ away from the stitching as shown and press the triangle back.

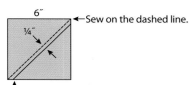

6. Mark a diagonal line on the wrong side of the 4″ × 4″ square.

7. With the right sides together, place the 4″ × 4″ square over the pieced 6″ × 6″ square as shown.

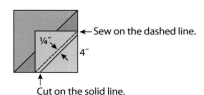

8. Sew on the marked line, cut ¼″ away from the stitching, and press the triangle back.

9. Repeat Steps 1–8 to make a total of 20 blocks.

Make 20.

what you need

FABRIC FOR BLOCKS: 40 different prints, each cut 10″ × 10″, or 10″ × 10″ precut pack

FABRIC FOR INNER AND OUTER BORDERS: ⅞ yard solid-color fabric

FABRIC FOR MIDDLE BORDER: fabric left over from 10″ squares

BINDING: ⅜ yard

BACKING FABRIC: 44″ × 50″

BATTING: 44″ × 50″

Rows

1. Sew together 4 blocks to make 1 row. Refer to the quilt assembly diagram (page 103) to make sure the blocks are turned in alternating directions. Press seam allowances in alternating directions on adjacent rows.

2. Make a total of 5 rows.

3. Sew together the 5 rows and press.

Borders

This quilt has an inner border, a middle border, and an outer border. Refer to Borders (page 136) to sew the strips to the sides, top, and bottom of the quilt, piecing them together to fit. When adding the middle border, press seam allowances toward the inner and outer borders.

1. Cut 3 strips 2″ × the width of the fabric from the solid fabric for the inner border.

2. Cut 26 strips 1½″ × 5″ from the fabric left from the blocks for the middle border. Randomly sew these pieces together along the 1½″ sides to make strips that fit the sides, top, and bottom of the quilt.

3. Cut 4 strips 5″ × the width of the fabric from the solid fabric for the outer border.

Finishing

For the binding, cut 5 pieces 2¼″ × the width of the fabric; sew them together using diagonal seams to make 1 long strip.

Refer to Basic Techniques (page 135) to layer, quilt, and bind the quilt.

Quilt your quilt top as desired. Our quilt features a clean, simple diagonal grid.

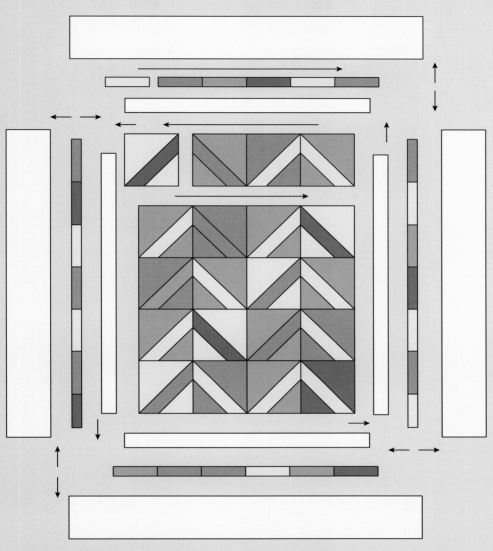

Quilt assembly diagram

RUFFLE PILLOW

Designed and made by Sweetwater

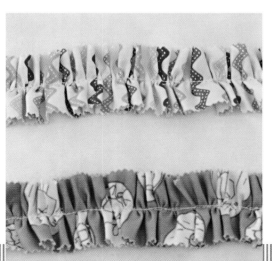

A rocking chair would be the perfect place for this pillow. Babies will love to feel the texture of the ruffles.

INSTRUCTIONS

A ¼″ seam allowance is included.

Pillow Front

1. Cut the background fabric 16½″ × 16½″.

2. Beginning 2¾″ from the lower edge, mark 5 lines 2¾″ apart across the width of the square. These lines will be the guide for the placement of the ruffles.

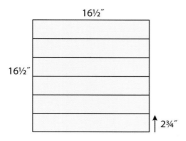

Mark guidelines for ruffles.

Ruffles

1. Sew a gathering stitch down the center of each 1½″ strip of ruffle fabric.

2. Pull the thread to gather the strip to measure 16½″.

3. Center the ruffles on the marked lines on the pillow front. Topstitch directly over the gathering stitching.

Pillow Back

1. Cut 2 pieces of background fabric 12½″ × 16½″ for the pillow back.

2. Refer to Pure Pillow under Pillow Assembly, Steps 2–6 (page 19), to finish the pillow.

what you need

FABRIC FOR BACK-GROUND: ½ yard

FABRIC FOR RUFFLES: 5 different prints, each cut 1½″ × width of fabric with small pinked edges

16″ × 16″ PILLOW FORM

FINISHED WALLHANGING:
30" × 5½"

DREAM WALLHANGING

Designed and made by Sweetwater

Easy-to-apply fabric labels make this project simple and quick. The sweet framed letters are designed to be hung from a curtain rod fastened to the wall; be sure to hang it well out of Baby's reach!

INSTRUCTIONS

A ¼″ seam allowance is included.

1. Cut 5 squares of canvas 4″ × 4″. With the right sides together, align the top right corner of a canvas square with a strip of border fabric. Sew the border print to the side of the square; trim away the excess strip. Press toward the border. Rotate the piece and sew the border strip to the remaining sides. Repeat for the other 4 canvas squares.

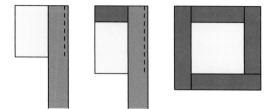

Sew border strip to 4″ square.

2. To make the fabric labels using a computer and iron-on inkjet-printable fabric, follow the instructions of the printable-fabric manufacturer to make labels measuring approximately 1½″ × either 1½″ or 2″, depending on the shape of the letter.

3. Peel off the paper backing (if there is one) from the labels and iron a label to the center of each piece.

4. Stitch close around the edge of each label.

5. Cut 5 pieces 6″ × 6″ of backing fabric. With the right sides together, center the front and backing pieces over the 6½″ × 6½″ batting squares.

6. Cut 10 pieces of ribbon 12″ long. Fold 2 pieces in half crosswise for each square.

7. Sandwich the folded edge of the ribbon in between the front and the backing at the top corners.

what you need

FABRIC FOR BACKGROUND: canvas fabric, cut 4″ × width of fabric

FABRIC FOR BORDERS: 5 different print fabrics, each cut 1½″ × width of fabric

5 IRON-ON FABRIC LETTER LABELS (see Resources, page 140) or 1 sheet iron-on inkjet-printable fabric

BACKING FABRIC: 6″ × width of fabric

BATTING: 5 pieces 6½″ × 6½″

¼″-WIDE RIBBON: 3½ yards

CURTAIN ROD: 36″ long with brackets to hang on wall

Helpful Hint

You can buy iron-on labels from Sweetwater that can be custom printed with any letters you choose. As an alternative to these, you can use inkjet-printable fabric with iron-on adhesive on the back.

8. Sew all the layers together, leaving a 2″ opening at the bottom of each. Be careful not to catch the ribbons in the seams.

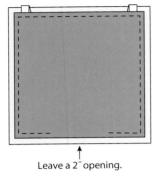

Leave a 2″ opening.

Sew all layers together.

9. Trim away the excess batting and trim the corners. Turn the pieces right side out through the openings.

10. Topstitch close to the edges. This will secure the openings closed.

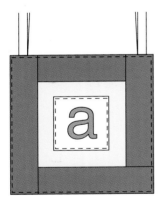

Topstitch around edges.

11. Attach the curtain rod to the wall and tie on the squares.

the GUEST ROOM

When decorating a guest room, incorporate items that will create a relaxing, serene environment and make your guests feel special. Make the bed with a warm, cozy handmade quilt, and prepare a basket filled with water bottles, toothpaste, and magazines. Small touches, such as a handwritten welcome note and towels tied up in ribbon, create big impressions.

GUEST THROW
QUILT

*Designed and made by Sweetwater
and machine quilted by Brian Clements*

On this dramatic quilt, the narrow pieced strips leave a nice, large area to showcase intricate quilting. If you want to make the coordinating Framed Wallhanging (page 118), make an extra strip of the pieced fabrics.

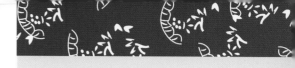

INSTRUCTIONS

A ¼″ seam allowance is included.

Pieced Strips

1. Cut 2 strips 1″ × the width of the fabric from each of the 16 prints.

2. With the right sides together, sew the 16 strips together along the long sides to make 2 strip sets.

3. Press the seams to one side.

4. Crosscut the strip sets to make a total of 25 sections 2″ wide as shown.

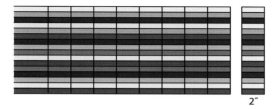

Crosscut strip sets to make 25 sections.

5. Sew 5 sections together along the 2″ sides to make a total of 5 strips. Each of the 5 strips will have 80 pieces. Press.

Sashing and Side Borders

1. Cut 6 pieces 6″ × 40½″ from the sashing and border fabric.

2. With the right sides together, sew the pieces to the pieced strips along the long edges as shown in the quilt assembly diagram (page 115). Press the seams toward the sashing and borders.

Top and Bottom Borders

1. Cut 2 pieces 6″ × 41″ from the sashing and border fabric.

2. Sew the pieces to the top and bottom of the quilt. Press.

what you need

FABRIC FOR PIECED STRIPS: 16 different prints, each cut 2″ × width of fabric

FABRIC FOR SASHING AND BORDERS: 1½ yards (minimum 42″ wide)

BINDING: ⅜ yard

BACKING FABRIC: 49″ × 59″

BATTING: 49″ × 59″

Finishing

For the binding, cut 5 strips 2¼″ wide × the width of the fabric; sew together using diagonal seams to make 1 long strip.

Refer to Basic Techniques (page 135) to layer, quilt, and bind the quilt.

Quilt your quilt top as desired. This quilt really shows off the quilting design. Ours is closely quilted in an allover flower pattern.

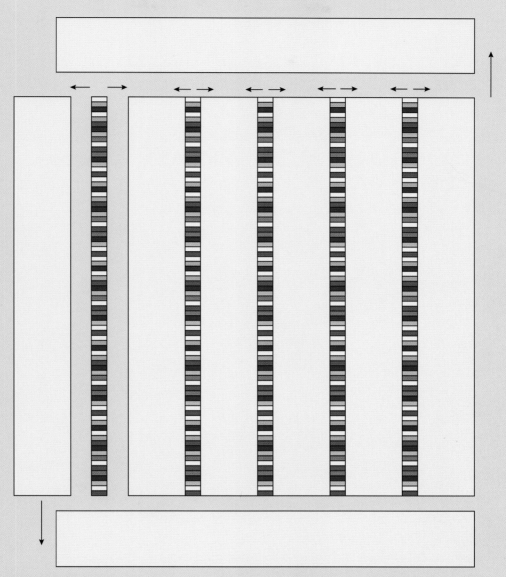

Quilt assembly diagram

BUTTON PILLOW

Designed and made by Sweetwater

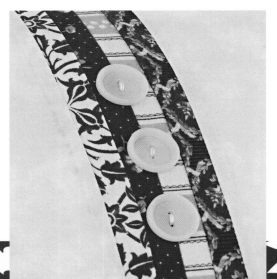

This pillow is super easy and a great complement to the Guest Throw Quilt (page 112).

INSTRUCTIONS

A ¼" seam allowance is included.

Front

1. With the right sides together, sew the 4 center strips together along the 12½" sides to make the center strip.

2. Press the seams to one side.

3. Cut 2 pieces 7½" × 12½" from the background fabric.

4. With the right sides together, sew a background piece to each side of the center strip along the 12½" sides.

5. Sew 3 buttons to the center of the pieced strips.

Back

1. Cut 2 pieces of background fabric 12½" × 12½" for the pillow back.

2. Refer to Pure Pillow under Pillow Assembly, Steps 2–6 (page 19), to finish the pillow.

FRAMED
WALLHANGING

Designed and made by Sweetwater

This wallhanging uses the same pieced strips as the Guest Throw Quilt (page 112). Save time by sewing an extra strip when making the quilt.

INSTRUCTIONS

A ¼" seam allowance is included.

Pieced Center

1. With the right sides together, sew the 16 strips together along the long sides to make a strip set.

2. Press the seams to one side.

3. Crosscut the strip set into 3 sections 2" wide as shown.

4. Sew the 3 sections together along the 2" sides to make the pieced center strip. Press.

Borders

1. Cut 2 pieces 2¾" × 2" from the border fabric.

2. With the right sides together, sew a piece to each end of the pieced center strip, along the 2" sides.

3. Cut 2 pieces 29" × 3½" from the border fabric.

4. With the right sides together, sew these pieces to the top and bottom of the pieced center.

Finishing

1. Layer the backing, batting, and top together.

2. Quilt as desired. Ours was quilted using a diagonal crosshatch pattern with the stitching lines 1" apart.

3. Trim away the excess backing and batting. Check that the piece fits your frame, and trim it to size if required.

4. Zigzag the outer edges to keep them from raveling.

5. Trace the opening edges onto the frame back. Apply double-stick carpet tape to the back of the frame along the traced edges on the back.

6. Remove the paper from the tape and position the wallhanging over the tape to secure it.

7. Insert the wallhanging into the frame.

Crosscut strip set into 3 sections.

FABRIC FOR CENTER STRIP:
16 different prints,
each cut 1" × 8"

FABRIC FOR BORDERS: ⅜ yard

BACKING FABRIC: 9" × 30"

BATTING: 9" × 30"

FRAME WITH 28" × 7" OPENING
(choose a frame with a back)

DOUBLE-STICK CARPET TAPE

EMBELLISHED SHEETS

These will be a special surprise for your guests—they'll probably wish they could take them home! In fact, you could even make a gift of them at the end of their stay.

INSTRUCTIONS

Top Sheet

1. Cut 2 or 3 strips (depending on the size of the sheets) 2½″ × the width of the fabric from the trim fabric.

2. With the right sides together, sew the strips together along the 2½″ sides to make 1 long strip.

3. Adjust the length of the strip to fit the width of the top sheet and add ½″.

4. Turn the strip under ¼″ on all sides and press.

5. Sew the strip to the right side of the sheet, placing the fabric 1″ from the top edge.

Pillowcases

The embroidery pattern is below.

To create the words for the embroidery, you can use the pattern provided or print the words using a computer. Try using a hand-writing font; many fonts are readily available for personal use on free font sites on the Internet. Make sure your phrase fits the pillowcase! You can also use your own handwriting for the pattern; use lined notebook paper to keep the writing even.

1. Copy the embroidery pattern below to make a template. Center the words for the embroidery on the hem of each pillowcase and trace them with a pencil. (You may need to use a lightbox or hold the pillowcase up to a window.)

2. With 2 strands of embroidery floss, embroider the words using a backstitch.

3. Sew a decorative running stitch close to the hem of the pillowcase with the embroidery floss.

the DINING ROOM

Food always brings people together. Whether it is Thanksgiving dinner or just an ordinary Tuesday night, make your dining experience special. Handmade table linens such as cloth napkins and a colorful table runner—plus cheerful patchwork signs on the wall—can turn any dinner into an event. Make all three projects in coordinating prints for a pulled-together look.

HALF-CIRCLES
TABLE RUNNER

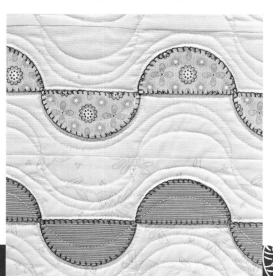

Designed and made by Sweetwater

Fused and appliquéd half-circles make this table runner a cinch to create. Try using this runner at breakfast—the colors in the appliqués and inner borders are so happy and energizing.

INSTRUCTIONS

A ¼″ seam allowance is included.

Background

1. Cut 2 pieces 18½″ × 5″ from each of the 3 neutral prints; there will be 6 total.

2. With the right sides together, sew the pieces together along the 18½″ sides, arranging the prints as shown. Press the seams to one side.

Fabric A
Fabric B
Fabric C
Fabric C
Fabric B
Fabric A

Appliqué

The pattern is on page 126.

1. Trace the circle and the cutting line from the pattern 18 times onto the paper side of the fusible web, leaving at least ½″ between the circles.

2. Cut out the circles, leaving a ¼″ margin around each. Iron 6 circles to the wrong side of each of the 3 appliqué prints, following the manufacturer's instructions.

3. Cut out the circles, and then cut each circle in half along the cutting line.

4. Peel off the paper backing and iron the half-circles to the center of each background strip, positioning the straight edges of the half-circles in the center of the strips as shown in the assembly diagram (page 126).

FABRIC FOR BACKGROUND: 3 light neutral prints, ¼ yard each*

FABRIC FOR HALF-CIRCLE APPLIQUÉS: 3 different prints, ⅛ yard each

FABRIC FOR INNER BORDER: 3 different prints, each cut 1″ × width of fabric

FABRIC FOR OUTER BORDER: ⅓ yard light neutral print fabric*

PAPER-BACKED FUSIBLE WEB: ½ yard

EMBROIDERY FLOSS

BINDING: ⅓ yard

BACKING FABRIC: 26″ × 45″

BATTING: 26″ × 45″

We used very light tone-on-tone neutrals, but you could also use solid neutral fabric.

5. Using 3 strands of embroidery floss, stitch a blanket stitch around the edges of each half-circle.

Borders

At each end of the table runner is an inner border pieced from 3 strips, and an outer border of neutral fabric.

1. Sew the print inner border strips together to make a strip set. Crosscut the strip set into 2 sections 18½" long.

2. Sew 1 inner border strip set to each end of the table runner.

3. Cut 2 pieces 4" × 18½" from the outer border fabric and sew 1 piece to each end of the table runner.

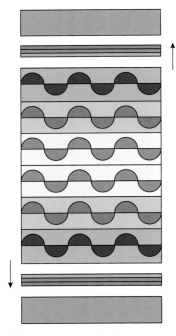

Table runner assembly diagram

Finishing

For the binding, cut 4 strips 2¼" × the width of the fabric; sew them together end to end, using diagonal seams, to make 1 long strip.

Refer to Basic Techniques (page 135) to layer, quilt, and bind the table runner.

Quilt your table runner as desired.

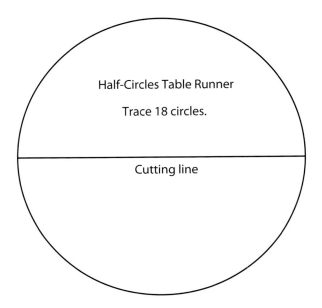

Half-Circles Table Runner

Trace 18 circles.

Cutting line

FINISHED NAPKIN:
17¼" × 17¼"

COLORFUL NAPKINS

Designed and made by Sweetwater

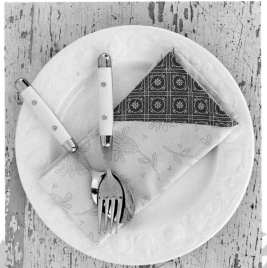

Cloth napkins make any meal feel special. With this easy pattern, you can make several.

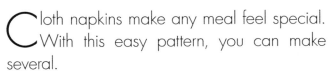

INSTRUCTIONS

A ¼" seam allowance is included. These instructions are for one napkin.

1. From the main fabric, cut 1 piece 18" × 18".

2. On the wrong side of the trim fabric, mark a diagonal line from corner to corner.

3. With the right sides together, place the trim square over a corner of the main fabric, matching the raw edges.

4. Sew the 2 layers together on the diagonal drawn line as shown.

5. Cut away the bottom section of the corner trim square ¼" down from the seam as shown.

6. Press the remaining trim triangle over the top of the main fabric. Baste the trim corner to the underlying main fabric and treat as 1 piece.

7. To prepare the mitered corners, turn a 1½" corner to the wrong side at each corner as shown and press. Trim the corners, leaving a ¼" seam allowance.

8. For the hem, turn the edges ⅜" to the wrong side around all 4 sides and press. Turn the edges ⅜" to the wrong side again, aligning the folded corner edges, and press.

9. Topstitch the hem in place.

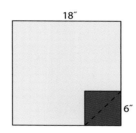

Sew on diagonal drawn line.

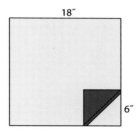

Cut away corner trim square.

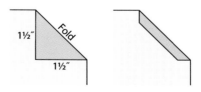

Fold 1½" corner and trim.

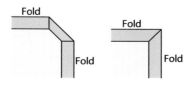

Turn edges ⅜" to wrong side twice.

what you need

Makes 2 napkins.

MAIN FABRIC: ½ yard

TRIM FABRIC: 2 prints, each cut 6" × 6"

PATCHWORK WALLHANGINGS

Designed and made by Sweetwater

Add a note of fun and welcome with this triptych of bright framed pieces for your wall. All three use 1″ strips for the piecing, but they are pieced together in different ways.

INSTRUCTIONS

The patterns are on page 133; a ¼″ seam allowance is included.

Good Food

1. Cut 12 strips 1″ × 14″ from the border fabric.

2. With the right sides together, sew the strips together along the long sides to make a strip set.

3. Press the seams to one side.

4. Crosscut the strip set into 6 sections 2″ wide as shown.

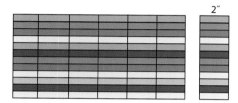

Crosscut strip set into 6 sections.

5. Sew 3 sections together along the 2″ sides to make each border.

6. Cut 1 piece 18½″ × 5½″ from the background fabric.

7. With the right sides together, sew the borders to the top and bottom of the background piece. Press the seams toward the borders.

8. Layer the backing, batting, and top together.

9. Quilt as desired. Ours was quilted using a diagonal crosshatch pattern with the stitching lines 1″ apart.

10. Trace the words "Good Food" from the pattern to make a template. Enlarge and copy the words 200% to make the finished template.

11. Trace around the words "Good Food" from the template onto the paper side of the fusible web.

12. Iron the fusible web to the wrong side of the fabric for the word appliqués, following the manufacturer's instructions.

13. Cut out the words on the traced lines, peel off the paper backing, and iron the words to the background fabric.

FABRIC FOR BACKGROUND OF LETTERING: 3 different prints, ¼ yard each

FABRIC FOR BORDERS: 12 or more different prints, each cut 1″ × width of fabric

FABRIC FOR WORD APPLIQUÉS: scraps

PAPER-BACKED FUSIBLE WEB: ½ yard

BACKING FABRIC: 3 pieces 9″ × 20″

COTTON BATTING: 3 pieces 9″ × 20″

3 FRAMES WITH 18″ × 8″ OPENINGS (choose frames that have backs)

DOUBLE-STICK CARPET TAPE

14. Machine stitch close to the edge of each
    word, using a straight stitch.

15. Check that the piece fits your frame and trim it to size if
    required. Zigzag the outer edges to keep them from raveling.

Good Friends

1. Cut 6 strips 1″ × 19″ from the border fabric.

2. With the right sides together, sew the strips together along
   the long sides to make a strip set.

3. Press the seams to one side.

4. Cut the strip set 18½″ long.

5. Cut 1 piece 5½″ × 18½″ from the background fabric.

6. With the right sides together, sew the border to the top of
   the background piece. Press the seam to one side.

7. Follow Steps 8–15 under Good Food (previous page),
   but use the words "Good Friends" instead.

Good Times

The instructions are the same as for the Good Friends wallhanging,
except the pieced border is sewn to the bottom of the background
piece, and we quilted this piece using vertical channel quilting with
the stitching lines 1″ apart.

Frames

1. Stitch close to the edges of the wallhangings.

2. Trace the opening edges onto the frame back. Apply double-stick
   carpet tape to the backs of the frames along the traced edges
   of the back.

3. Remove the paper from the tape and position the wallhangings
   over the tape to secure them.

4. Insert the wallhangings into the frames.

good

FOOD

TIMES

FRIENDS

Enlarge 200%.

BASIC TECHNIQUES

GENERAL GUIDELINES

Seam Allowances

A ¼″ seam allowance is used for most projects. It's a good idea to do a test seam before you begin sewing to check that your ¼″ is accurate. Accuracy is the key to successful piecing.

There is no need to backstitch when seamlines will be crossed by another seam that will anchor them.

Pressing

In general, press seams toward the darker fabric. Press lightly in an up-and-down motion. Avoid using a very hot iron or over-ironing, which can distort shapes and blocks. Be especially careful when pressing bias edges, as they stretch easily.

BORDERS

When border strips are cut on the crosswise grain, piece the strips together to achieve the needed lengths.

Butted Borders

In most cases the side borders are sewn on first. When you have finished the quilt top, measure it through the center vertically. This will be the length to cut the side borders. Place pins at the centers of all four sides of the quilt top, as well as in the center of each side border strip. Pin the side borders to the quilt top first, matching the center pins. Using a ¼″ seam allowance, sew the borders to the quilt top and press toward the border.

Measure horizontally across the center of the quilt top, including the side borders. This will be the length to cut the top and bottom borders. Repeat, pinning, sewing, and pressing.

BACKING

Plan on making the backing approximately 8″ longer and wider than the quilt top. Backings for smaller projects can be 2″ to 3″ larger. Piece, if necessary. Trim the selvages before you piece to the desired size.

To economize, piece the back from any leftover quilting fabrics or blocks in your collection.

BATTING

The type of batting to use is a personal decision; consult your local quilt shop. Cut batting the same size as the backing fabric. Note that your batting choice will affect how much quilting is necessary for the quilt. Check the manufacturer's instructions to see how far apart the quilting lines can be.

LAYERING

Spread the backing wrong side up and tape the edges down with masking tape. (If you are working on carpet you can use T-pins to secure the backing to the carpet.) Center the batting on top and smooth out any folds. Place the quilt top right side up on top of the batting and backing, making sure it is centered.

BASTING

Basting keeps the quilt "sandwich" layers from shifting while you are quilting.

If you plan to machine quilt, pin baste the quilt layers together with safety pins placed a minimum of 3″–4″ apart. Begin basting in the center and move toward the edges, first in vertical, then horizontal, rows. Try not to pin directly on the intended quilting lines.

If you plan to hand quilt, baste the layers together with thread using a long needle and light-colored thread. Knot one end of the thread. Using stitches approximately the length of the needle, begin in the center and move out toward the edges in vertical and horizontal rows approximately 4″ apart. Add two diagonal rows of basting.

QUILTING

Quilting, whether by hand or machine, enhances the pieced or appliquéd design of the quilt. You may choose to quilt in-the-ditch, echo the pieced or appliqué motifs, use patterns from quilting design books and stencils, or do your own free-motion quilting. Remember to check the batting manufacturer's recommendations for how close the quilting lines must be.

BINDING

Trim excess batting and backing even with the edges of the quilt top.

Double-Fold Straight-Grain Binding

Cut the binding strips and piece them together with diagonal seams to make a continuous binding strip. Trim the seam allowance to ¼″. Press the seams open.

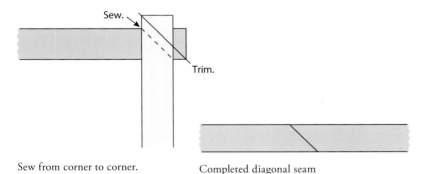

Sew from corner to corner.   Completed diagonal seam

Press the entire strip in half lengthwise with wrong sides together. With raw edges even, pin the binding to the front edge of the quilt a few inches away from the corner, and leave the first few inches of the binding unattached. Start sewing, using a ¼″ seam allowance.

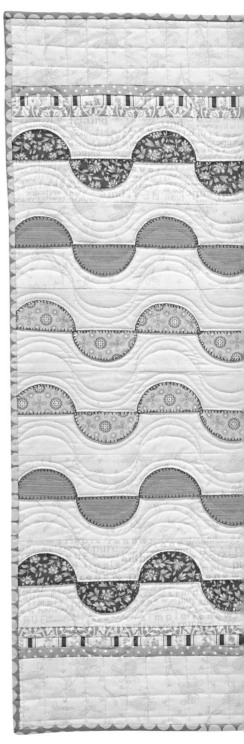

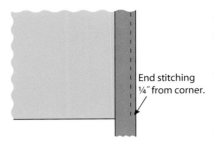

Step 1. Stitch to ¼" from corner.

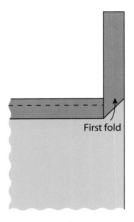

Step 2. First fold for miter

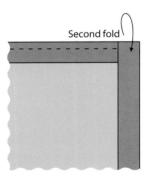

Step 3. Second fold alignment

Stop ¼" away from the first corner (see Step 1) and backstitch one stitch. Lift the presser foot and needle. Rotate the quilt one-quarter turn. Fold the binding at a right angle so it extends straight above the quilt and the fold forms a 45° angle in the corner (see Step 2). Then bring the binding strip down even with the edge of the quilt (see Step 3). Begin sewing at the folded edge. Repeat in the same manner at the remaining corners.

Continue stitching until you are back near the beginning of the binding strip. See Finishing the Binding Ends for tips on finishing and hiding the raw edges of the ends of the binding.

Continuous Bias Binding

A continuous bias involves using a square sliced in half diagonally and then sewing the triangles together so that you continuously cut marked strips to make continuous bias binding. The same instructions can be used to cut bias for piping.

Cut the fabric for the bias binding or piping so it is a square. For example, if yardage is ½ yard, cut an 18" × 18" square. Cut the square in half diagonally, creating two triangles.

Sew these triangles together as shown, using a ¼" seam allowance. Press the seam open.

Using a ruler, mark the parallelogram created by the two triangles with lines spaced the width you need to cut the bias. Cut about 5" along the first line.

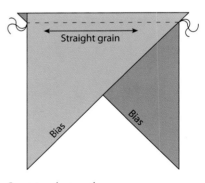

Sew triangles together.

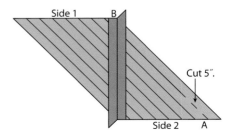

Mark lines and begin cutting.

Join side 1 and side 2 to form a tube. The raw edge at line A will align with the raw edge at B. This will allow the first line to be offset by one strip width. Pin the raw edges right sides together, making sure that the lines match. Sew with a ¼″ seam allowance. Press the seam open. Cut along the drawn lines, creating one continuous strip.

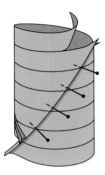

Press the entire strip in half lengthwise with wrong sides together. Place the binding on the quilt as described above in Double-Fold Straight-Grain Binding.

See Finishing the Binding Ends for tips on finishing and hiding the raw edges of the ends of the binding.

Finishing the Binding Ends

Method 1

After stitching around the quilt, fold under the beginning tail of the binding strip ¼″ so that the raw edge will be inside the binding after it is turned to the back side of the quilt. Place the end tail of the binding strip over the beginning folded end. Continue to attach the binding and stitch slightly beyond the starting stitches. Trim the excess binding. Fold the binding over the raw edges to the quilt back and hand stitch, mitering the corners.

Method 2

See our blog entry at ctpubblog.com; search for "invisible seam," and then scroll down to "Quilting Tips: Completing a Binding with an Invisible Seam."

Fold the ending tail of the binding back on itself where it meets the beginning binding tail. From the fold, measure and mark the cut width of the binding strip. Cut the ending binding tail to this measurement. For example, if the binding is cut 2⅛″ wide, measure from the fold on the ending tail of the binding 2⅛″ and cut the binding tail to this length.

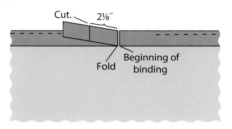

Cut binding tail.

Open both tails. Place one tail on top of the other tail at right angles, right sides together. Mark a diagonal line from corner to corner and stitch on the line. Check that you've done it correctly and that the binding fits the quilt, and then trim the seam allowance to ¼″. Press open.

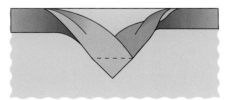

Stitch ends of binding diagonally.

Refold the binding and stitch this binding section in place on the quilt. Fold the binding over the raw edges to the quilt back and hand stitch.

RESOURCES

Fabrics and Other Materials

THE ENTRYWAY

- Quilt and pillow fabrics: *Pure* by Sweetwater for Moda

- White frame with black words: Hobby Lobby

THE KITCHEN

- Apron, placemat, and pot holder fabrics (black and cream): *Authentic* by Sweetwater for Moda

- Trim fabric: MoMo for Moda

THE OFFICE

- Birthday board, lamp, chair, and notebook cover fabrics: *Authentic* by Sweetwater for Moda

- Iron-on fabric labels (for birthday board): Sweetwater

THE MASTER SUITE

- Quilt and pillow fabrics: French General for Moda

- Toiletry bag and towel fabrics: *Authentic* by Sweetwater for Moda

- Tray liner fabrics: *Authentic* by Sweetwater for Moda, and *Mill House Inn* by Fig Tree and Co. for Moda

THE LAUNDRY ROOM

- Laundry hamper, clothespin bag, and jar label fabrics: French General for Moda

- Iron-on fabric labels (for jar labels): Sweetwater

THE FAMILY ROOM

- Quilt, floor cushions, and checkerboard fabrics: *Make Life* by Sweetwater for Moda

THE BABY ROOM

- Quilt, pillow, and wallhanging fabrics: *Whimsy* by Fig Tree and Co. for Moda

- Iron-on fabric labels (for wallhanging): Sweetwater

THE GUEST ROOM

- Quilt, wallhanging, and pillow fabrics: *Simple Abundance* by Bonnie and Camille for Moda

- Sheet fabrics: *Simple Abundance* by Bonnie and Camille for Moda

THE DINING ROOM

- Table runner and wallhanging fabrics: *Simple Abundance* by Bonnie and Camille for Moda

Ordering Information for Iron-On Labels

To order any of the labels for the Birthday Board, Notepad Covers, Organizer Jar Labels, or Dream Wallhanging, please visit sweetwaterstreet.com or call 970-867-4428.

Contact Information

The following are websites, email addresses, blogs, and telephone numbers of designers and manufacturers whose products were used in this book.

SWEETWATER

WEBSITES: sweetwaterscrapbook.com; sweetwaterstreet.com

BLOG: sweetwater.typepad.com

EMAIL: info@sweetwaterscrapbook.com

PHONE: 970-867-4428

COTTON WAY

Bonnie Olvaeson

WEBSITE: cottonway.com

BLOG: cottonway.blogspot.com

EMAIL: bonnie@cottonway.com

PHONE: 208-745-6742

FRENCH GENERAL

Kaari Meng

WEBSITE: frenchgeneral.com

BLOG: frenchgeneral.blogspot.com

EMAIL: notions@frenchgeneral.com

PHONE: 323-668-0488

FIG TREE AND CO.

Joanna Figueroa

WEBSITE: figtreequilts.com

BLOG: figtreequilts.typepad.com

EMAIL: joanna@figtreequilts.com

PHONE: 510-632-5358

MODA FABRICS / UNITED NOTIONS

WEBSITE: unitednotions.com

EMAIL: service@unitednotions.com

PHONE: 800-527-9447

THIMBLE BLOSSOMS

Camille Roskelley

WEBSITE: thimbleblossoms.com

BLOG: camilleroskelley.typepad.com

EMAIL: camille@thimbleblossoms.com

PHONE: 702-673-7161

For a list of other fine books from C&T Publishing, visit our website to view our catalog online.

C&T PUBLISHING, INC.
P.O. Box 1456
Lafayette, CA 94549
800-284-1114

Email: ctinfo@ctpub.com
Website: www.ctpub.com

C&T Publishing's professional photography services are now available to the public. Visit us at www.ctmediaservices.com.

Tips and Techniques can be found at www.ctpub.com > Consumer Resources > Quiltmaking Basics: Tips & Techniques for Quiltmaking & More

For quilting supplies:

COTTON PATCH
1025 Brown Ave.
Lafayette, CA 94549
Store: 925-284-1177
Mail order: 925-283-7883

Email: CottonPa@aol.com
Website: www.quiltusa.com

ABOUT THE AUTHORS

Sweetwater is a family-run business consisting of a mom and her two daughters. However, the company didn't actually begin as "Sweetwater."

In 1985 Karla Eisenach went into a fabric shop carrying a handmade fabric basket and the instructions to make it. The store owner loved it, and a pattern company was launched. Because Karla lived in rural Colorado on a farm, she named the company Farmyard Creations. For more than 20 years, she has designed hundreds of patterns, including patterns for quilts, bags, and table runners.

In 2001, her daughters, Susan and Lisa, decided to take on a big challenge and start a scrapbook business called Sweetwater. They began designing, marketing, and selling patterned paper and scrapbook embellishments to hundreds of stores across the United States and abroad. The demands of the scrapbook industry were great, and Karla took a break from the quilting business to focus on the new venture.

Seven years later, the three women were given the opportunity to design a fabric collection for Moda. Karla was more than happy to get back to sewing, and Lisa and Susan needed a break from designing hundreds of scrapbooking products. Because the fabric designing is a joint venture, they kept the name Sweetwater and currently sell quilt patterns under that name.